THINKING MINDS

NUANCES OF LIFE THROUGH DIVERSE CULTURES

DR SINDHU VASANTH B | ZIDAN KACHHI | LIKITHA S (EDS.)

Contents

Contents

Preface

Cross-cultural psychology is not merely an academic discipline; it is a critical lens through which we can better understand the diverse and interconnected world we live in. The insights gained from cross-cultural psychology assignments reveal the intricate ways in which culture shapes our thoughts, emotions, behaviors, and interactions. This book is a culmination of such explorations and aims to provide students, researchers, and practitioners with a comprehensive foundation in this essential field. This book is the result of collaborative efforts from students, educators and consulting psychologists who have contributed their insights and experiences through various cross-cultural psychology assignments. Their dedication and passion for understanding cultural diversity have enriched this work and made it a valuable resource for anyone seeking to navigate the complexities of our multicultural world. We hope that this book will inspire readers to appreciate the richness of cultural diversity and to apply cross-cultural psychology principles in their academic, professional, and personal lives.

- Dr Sindhu Vasanth B

About The Editors

Dr Sindhu Vasanth B (Counselling Psychologist)

Assistant Professor, PES University, Bengaluru, India

Dr Sindhu Vasanth B is a seasoned educator, trainer, and counsellor with over 12 years of experience. Holding a PhD from University of Mysore. She has completed her MPhil in Psychology and an MSc in Psychological Counselling (4th rank in Bangalore University). She has served on the interview panel for the Karnataka State Police and has delivered guest lectures and training programmes on various topics related to mental health, published research on classroom interaction, and is a Life Member of the Counsellor Council of India (CCI).

***

Zidan Kachhi (Counselling Psychologist)

Assistant Professor, PES University, Bengaluru, India

Mr Zidan Kachhi is a dedicated Counselling Psychologist, Assistant Professor, Researcher, Author, and Trainer with over five years in psychology and more than two years in teaching and training. He is currently pursuing a PhD in Psychology. Deeply committed to advancing knowledge and practice, his work prioritises individual contexts, intersectionality, and inclusivity in counselling, organisational settings, and academia. As a Queer Affirmative practitioner, fostering an inclusive therapeutic environment is paramount to him. He utilises an integrative approach and is trained in Couple and Family Therapy and Transactional Analysis. With multidisciplinary collaboration, he contributes to enhancing individual and collective well-being through research, education, and practice.

***

Likitha S (Forensic Psychologist)

Assistant Professor, PES University, Bengaluru, India

Ms Likitha S has a diverse range of work experience in her domain. She has pursued an MSc in Psychology from Surana College, Bengaluru and an MPhil in Forensic Psychology from the National Forensic Sciences University, Gujarat. She has also worked with the Indian Institute of Science. Her expertise and research interests include psychopathy, serial killings, vicitimization, child abuse and childhood trauma.

Disclaimer

The views and opinions expressed in this book are those of the individual authors and do not necessarily reflect the official policy or position of the editors or the publishing institution. The authors are responsible for the accuracy, authenticity, and originality of their work, including any issues related to plagiarism or copyright infringement. The editors and the publishing institution bear no responsibility for any errors, omissions, or legal issues that may arise from the content of this book. By including these chapters, the editors are providing a platform for student work and are not endorsing the content or the viewpoints presented. All authors have provided their consent for their work to be published in this book.

CHAPTER ONE

Cultural Mosaic: An Introduction to Cross-Cultural Psychology

- Dr Sindhu Vasanth B

Background

Do you believe in lucky charms, horseshoes, rabbit's foot, lucky numbers, godmen, fortune tellers, having curd before going out to do an auspicious thing etc? Does all of these and numerous other superstitious beliefs startle you? Do you still believe some of these or in the process of rationalizing or blindly follow it because you are asked to?

Life encompasses wide array of diversities. The diversities are shaped by the set of values, principles, morals and ways of living that influence the way we think about each individual and the society in which we inhabit. These diversities make each individual unique, with this uniqueness stemming from the subjective experiences and perceptions about people and the society in large. The similar experiences and perceptions embrace the people to form the foundations of culture. The subjective experiences shape the lifestyle, attitudes, beliefs and norms of individual. Culture underscores the meaning of understanding human behaviour. The behaviour encompasses cultural contexts in forming and shaping the individual identity and behaviours. Berry, Poortinga, Segall, and Dasen (2002) defined culture as "the shared way of life of a group of people". Culture is dubious in nature which instigates the changes in perception and behaviour within the individuals and the groups. The analogies and disparities in the way individual and the individuals in the group behave form the basis of cross- cultural psychology.

The aim of cross-cultural psychology is to uncover the various constructs of culture and not universalising culture and cultural practices. The cultural practices vividly entail the symbols, practices, identities, customs, experiences which could be classified as implicit and explicit. The observable characteristics which explain the behaviour is called an explicit (e.g. Namaste) whereas implicit characteristics are the constructs that guide human behaviour (e.g. unspoken rules). Knowledge and meanings that are shared between individuals give rise to a collection of routine activities that also serve to define culture (Scribner & Cole, 1981)

Approaches to Cross Cultural Psychology

The term "cultural evolution" refers to the process by which cultural practices, beliefs, and conventions undergo changes and growth over the course of time. The evolutionary approach focused on adopting to the environment for survival. Charles Darwin further developed the concept of survival through his theory of natural selection. The members of the group need to required skill set to survive and to pass on survival traits to one's offspring. This process is influenced by social, environmental, technological, and economic changes. The changes in social milieu some aspects of culture become more uniform across the globe, others merge to form new, hybrid cultures. The other aspects like the rise of social media, digital communications, the economic disparities and cultural sensitivity have added new facets of understanding the culture across the world. In the realm of psychological research understanding the significant challenges faced by the researcher in unfolding the concept of WEIRD is crucial. WEIRD is an acronym of Western, Educated, Industrialised, Rich and Democratic society anchors various aspects of culture. People who are considered "weird" stand out due to their unique characteristics when compared to other species. These people cover a wide range of domains, such as "visual perception, fairness, cooperation, spatial reasoning, moral reasoning, reasoning styles, self-concepts, related motivations, and the heritability of IQ" (Hwang, 2014). The second multilayered approach to culture is anthropological perspective which camouflage the influences of cultures being passed from one generation to other. This emphasises on the recognition of human culture which gives scope on understanding the complexities of dynamic and constantly evolving perceptions of human behaviour. It overshadows that culture is a learnt phenomenon. The Structural Functional Perspective is the third one to span cross-cultural psychology. This throws light on understanding cultural institutions like the family units, religion, social roles to achieve stability in functioning of human being and society. The diverse viewpoints presented are a method of establishing a shared comprehension of the way individuals are influenced by the unspoken norms that dictate the beliefs of a culture.

Strong Ties versus Weak Ties

The strong ties versus the weak ties is a concept popularly termed as collectivism versus individualism. The extent of adherence to established norms, customs values and traditions by individuals defines traditional and nontraditional cultures (Shiraev & Levy, 2020). Traditional cultures give prominence to established practices and customs followed and passed on by generations. E.g Monogamy. Nontraditional cultures allow individuals to have more autonomy over their personal choices and the way of living not being bound to any institution or any governing rituals/principles. E.g. open marriages. The ongoing debate of which influences the human behaviour intrigues the psychologist to ferret every strand of culture. Many cultures in India, China, Nigeria, Fiji etc claim interconnectedness, social harmony, interdependence as the basis of functioning in a society. These collectivist cultures share a common goal and prioritize group needs over the individual needs in the society. Conversely, those who prioritize the requirements of the individual over those of the group or society are referred to as individualistic. This refers to the cultural dimensions on how people identify their roles in their society when compared to the extent to which they can follow and adhere to the established norms, customs and traditions. Therefore, redefining the cultural imperatives based on individual's impositions of life and society.

Echoes of 11 Deaths: Ethos of Culture on Burari's

Mass Suicide!!! The mysterious death of 11 people in Delhi. Chundawat's were a middle-class family, well-knit joint Indian family. The three generations lived together, educated and having a good social stance in the society.

On the first of July 2018, the neighbours where surprised when the grocery shop owned by them was not opened which usually would by 5:30 AM. This alarmed the curious neighbours when they did not collect milk from the milkman. They went upstairs to find out and found that nine members of the family were blindfolded found hanging in a circular position and the 10th member opposite to the family. And the old lady, the mother of Lalit Chundawat (the youngest son) who was considered the decision-making authority of after his father's death in the family. As usual the patriarchy was followed in their family. A member of the criminal branch had expressed the opinion that the diaries' language was conversational, authoritative, and instructive. The family had to follow the directions on the last page of the diary, and those instructions led to a horrific occurrence.

On September 7, 2007, Lalit instructed his family to keep Bhopal Singh's black-and-white portrait visible as a reminder of him, which is the first time Bhopal Singh is mentioned in his diaries. The case unfolded or It was written in September, "Mann mein dhyan yahi rakho ki Daddy meri purani aadatein chhut jaye" [I hope you break your old habits].

The last item in the diary, made on June 24, 2018, detailed a seven-day ritual called the "Banyan Tree Ritual" that would accompany the puja known as Badh Puja. In its natural state, badh is a tree whose roots dangle from its branches. The occurrence was recorded in the diary at a certain time, purportedly around 1 AM.

There were specific instructions for the Badh Puja, including;

It was customary to perform the ritual for seven days straight; the puja was to be held the day after any guests had visited the family.

No outsiders visiting the residence were to be allowed to see anything associated with the puja, as per the instructions.

When performing the puja, it is best to utilize dim light and close your eyes entirely (as cited in Mahawar, S.,2022, January 19).

Psychological considerations abound while trying to make sense of Lalit Chundawat's actions in the Burrari case. These include, but are not limited to, the possibility of mental health concerns, the effects of trauma, and the role that cultural and societal dynamics played. Delusions and hallucinations, as well as Lalit's following ritualistic habits, suggest he may have been conversing with his dead father. Disorders such as severe bipolar illness or schizophrenia frequently accompany these symptoms. It is possible that Lalit's profound emotional dependence lies at the root of his unresolved anguish over his father's death and his subsequent belief in his father's spiritual existence. As a family, they wanted to keep in touch with the father who had passed away, and his reliance on her probably drove his behavior and their obedience.

Exploring Positions in Cross cultural Psychology using Hofstede's Cultural Dimensions

Hofstede's Cultural Dimensions aids cross-cultural psychologists in comprehending the impact of cultural values on behaviours and attitudes. Each dimension distinguishes the impact of culture. Let us explore each one of it in detail.

Power Distance Index (PDI)

The execution of power in the society between the individuals, people's acceptance of power is defined as Power Distance Index. The power dynamics brings in the chain of command and reactions between the leader and the follower which changes the structure of the society. The cultural acceptance of power reinforces the authority endorsing privileges, honours and legitimacy of power in society.

E.g The Burari case starkly illustrates how family power dynamics led to tragic outcome of 11 deaths in the family. The hierarchical structures played a significant role in the planning of mass suicide. The patriarch of the family (Lalit Chundawat) exerted rituals which led to mass ritualistic suicide.

Individualism Versus Collectivism (IDV)

The etic and emic methods are complementary and can be used to study individualism vs. collectivism (IDV). When it comes to cultural distinctions and universal patterns, the etic method provides a framework. On the other hand, the emic approach delves further into the specific context of how these cultural aspects are experienced inside different cultures. Cultural issues associated with individualism and collectivism can be better understood by combining the two perspectives.

E.g: In Burari case, the emic approach emphasizes on the family rituals, beliefs, symbols and power that obscured the ability of reasoning by the family members. On the other hand, the etic approach highlights the viewpoint of an outsider who followed cultural imperatives without questioning.

The tendency to view one's culture superior which led to ethnocentrism was clearly highlighted in the context of Burari's Case. The cultural lens that blindfolded the family members about mental health, superstitions, power dynamics etc that led to mishaps that could never be unturned.

Masculinity Versus Femininity (MAS)

The roles and responsibilities defined for men and women in the society. The culture demonstrates the masculine and feminine traits to provide deeper understanding about the way society functions. The gender roles were a ready reckoner to provide stability in the society. Unfortunately, the resulting anarchy has necessitated the constantly need of redefining and adjusting gender roles to fit different contexts

E.g. The patriarchal society was highlighted in Burari Case, where there was autonomy given to any women in the family. Lalit Chundawat's mother and his wife had no say over Lalit's directives. This leaves alarmed questioning on the existence of women and other family members who supported the authority, hierarchy and masculinity.

Uncertainty Avoidance Index (UAI)

The cultural influence on uncertainty. If they realize they can't control their own destiny, giving up will be an easy choice. It shows how much a culture's adherents value order and predictability over unpredictability and feel frightened by ambiguous or unclear circumstances. Rules and regulations provide stability, order and help in minimizing the risks involved in ambiguity.

E.g. The family's participation in the ritualistic practices can be seen as a coping mechanism of uncertainty. Mr. Lalit's directives were never questioned which could be possibly stemming from the need to comply to the self-proclaimed authority figure of the family.

Long Versus Short-term Orientation

The culture or the cultural aspect that would reap immediate or long-term rewards. This component looks at a culture's preference for immediate results, tradition, and upholding social duties versus long-term planning, perseverance, and thrift .(Examples of Cultural Dimensions, n.d.)

E.g. A combination of long-term and short-term thinking is on display in the Burari case. In their dedication to spiritual activities for future advantages, the family's extreme acts show a long-term orientation. On the other hand, their behaviour is focused on managing immediate concerns and adhering to conventional customs, which accords with a short-term orientation.

Indulgence Versus Restraint (IVR)

The Indulgence Versus Restraint (IVR) dimension, another of Hofstede's cultural dimensions. This dimension explores how cultures influence individual behaviors and societal norms by promoting or suppressing the fulfilment of needs and desires.

E.g Lalit Chundawat's directives illustrates a strong adherence to traditional norms and a sense of duty, characteristic of a restrained culture. The ritual was an act of fulfilling one's own desire through restrained culture. The constant need to be heard and exercising control was observed.

Conclusion

How cultural environments impact psychological processes and actions is laid forth in the first chapter of cross-cultural psychology. This chapter emphasizes the significance of cultural variances in psychology study and practice by outlining important features such as individualism versus collectivism, uncertainty avoidance, indulgence versus constraint, and techniques like emic and etic approaches. For successful worldwide communication, intercultural competence development, and culturally sensitive treatment of psychiatric disorders, an awareness of these cultural distinctions is essential.

References

Berry, J. W., Poortinga, Y. H., Segall, M. H., & Dasen, P. R. (2002). Cross-cultural psychology: Research and applications (2nd ed.). Cambridge University Press.

Cole, M. (1990). Cultural psychology: A once and future discipline? In J. J. Bergman (Ed.), Nebraska Symposium on Motivation, 1989: Cross-Cultural Perspectives (Vol. 37, pp. 279–336). Lincoln: University of Nebraska Press

Examples of Cultural Dimensions. (n.d.). https://www.asha.org/practice-portal/professional-issues/cultural-responsiveness/examples-of-cultural-dimensions/#:~:text=The%20long-%20versus%20short-term

Hwang, K. (2014). Cultural System vs. Pan-cultural Dimensions: Philosophical Reflection on Approaches for Indigenous Psychology. Journal for the Theory of Social Behaviour, 45(1), 2–25. https://doi.org/10.1111/jtsb.12051

Jiao J, Zhao J. Individualism, Collectivism, and Allocation Behavior: Evidence from the Ultimatum Game and Dictator Game. Behav Sci (Basel). 2023 Feb 14;13(2):169. doi: 10.3390/bs13020169. PMID: 36829398; PMCID: PMC9951955.

Mahawar, S. (2022, January 19). Burari death case: an insight - iPleaders. iPleaders. https://blog.ipleaders.in/burari-death-case-insight/

Scribner, S., & Cole, M. (1981). The psychology of literacy. Cambridge, MA: Harvard University Press.

Shiraev, E. B., & Levy, D. A. (2020). Cross-Cultural Psychology. Routledge.

Stankov, L., & Lee, J. (2009). Dimensions of cultural differences: Pancultural, ETIC/EMIC, and ecological approaches. Learning and Individual Differences, 19(3),

339–354. https://doi.org/10.1016/j.lindif.2008.09.003

Triandis, H. C. (1995). Individualism and collectivism. Westview Press.

CHAPTER TWO

Contours of Reflection: Cultural Paradigms in Self-Concept

- **Pratham M**

Background

The Conundrum of the self is mysterious. In Classic Literature, we see many interconnected concepts, such as Identity, Consciousness and Self other. The ideas of Western and Eastern understanding of self are diametrically contrasting. The Structural model for the mental apparatus, for instance, was proposed by Sigmund Freud is inclusive of the ego but it does not completely encompass the idea of self. According to Carl Jung the self-conception which is also known as individuation is the integration of the mask and the persona. This process entails identification or acknowledgement of persona, the shadow, anima or animus, and what is known as the Self which is the knitting point of the whole personality. According to Hegel, the self itself was divided into a dialectical process and pointed out that the self-identity came from the recognition of others.

Taking this into account, the question of the status of the human nature calls for a fresh linguistic-philosophical examination in light of both modern science and psychology. Today, neurosciences and neuropsychology are looking for the material basis of the self in the brain. Nonetheless, the usage of ambiguous concepts creates language uncertainty, which hinders this process.

The domain of how culture builds people's Self-images has been one of the central issues that the psychology and social sciences are interested in. Self-concept refers to the view that people have of themselves in regard to other people and the surrounding world and this is not a stranger to culture, norms, values and practices. Cultural settings are structures that give meaning and orientation to people's existence in the world, and guide their perception, action and interaction with other people. The purpose of this chapter is to describe and elaborate on a relationship between culture and self-constructs and analyze the differences between various cultural groups in the aspects of self-image, self-regard, and identity formation. Through exploring these cultural subtleties, this research intends to broaden understanding of people's complex individuality and contribute to development of culture-centered paradigms in psychology and other fields.

Ideas of self vary among cultures and time frames in terms of how much they are group-based versus independently, and how much they are reliant on collecting, performing, or accomplishing certain things. It has been demonstrated that these divergent views of oneself have widespread impacts on consumer behaviour, leading to a larger role for goods in defining identity in complex modern nations. People's general self-evaluation tends to differ systematically between cultures; such that, average levels of Self-concept appear to differ among civilizations. These differences appear to arise, at least partially, from the greater emphasis put on the formation of good self-esteem among Western cultures opposed to non-civilizations, notably countries in East Asia.

Cultural Differences in Self-concept

The degree to which identity is generated from individual qualities and behaviours versus collective features and activities is one fundamental distinction in ideas of self. This level resembles idea of "group" in certain ways (Douglas, 1970) . We also are familiar with determining the identity of ourselves and others through personal qualities such as age, employment, conduct, and different material markers of individual status in current Western societies. We also draw judgments about identification on group characteristics such as familial origin, national historical achievement, and public markers of cultural rank, but to a far lower extent (e.g., museums). In certain cultures and periods, common bases for identity predominates over personal attributes.

In these cultures, individuals are conscious of themselves as part of a coherent whole, whether it's a family, clan, or nation (Doob, 1960). Conceptualizes a hierarchy of self-constructs, ranging from the individual and concrete psyche to the impartial and abstract mega-self. The focus is often on the hierarchy's more intimate levels (Atkin, 1981).

The bulk of primitive civilizations illustrate group ideas of self-most vividly. Similarly observed the absence of ego-consciousness in prehistoric man, demonstrated by the collective usage of the plural "we" in many primitive languages, even when referring to individual actions or ownership (Kelson ,1943). The literature reveals substantial variation in Self-concept across different cultures. Self-concept is not universal but varies across cultures, distinguishing between independent self-construal (focusing on personal attributes, abilities, and achievements) and interdependent self-construal (focusing on social roles, relationships, and obligations) (Markus & Kitayama, 1991). This distinction is supported, who developed a measure of independent and interdependent self-construal widely used in cross-cultural studies (Singelis, 1994). Western cultures tend to emphasize individuality and uniqueness, while East Asian cultures emphasize social harmony and conformity. This cultural difference may lead to differences in Self-concept , as individuals in Western cultures may describe themselves in terms of their unique qualities, while individuals in East Asian cultures may describe themselves in terms of their social relationships and obligations (Kim & Markus, 1999). However, the dichotomy between collectivism and individualism is not always clear-cut. Individuals in collectivistic cultures may still value personal achievement and self-expression, and those in individualistic cultures may prioritize social relationships and obligations (Oyserman et al., 2002).

Tsai & Chentsova-Dutton (2010) explored the role of culture in emotional reactivity and found that individuals from interdependent cultures (such as East Asian cultures) are more likely to manage their emotions in response to social cues, whereas individuals from independent cultures (like Western cultures) are more likely to regulate their emotions according to their personal goals and beliefs. Triandis (1995) differentiates between horizontal and vertical collectivism and individualism. Vertical individualism and collectivism refer to the extent to which individuals see themselves in relation to those in positions of authority or power, while horizontal individualism and collectivism refer to the extent to which individuals see themselves in relation to their peers. Choi et al (1999) examined cultural variations in causal attribution, finding that individuals in Western cultures tend to attribute behaviour to dispositional factors (such as personality traits), while individuals in East Asian cultures are more likely to attribute behaviour to situational factors (such as social norms or context). The intersection of cultural factors and gender in Self-concept , finding that women in individualistic cultures are more likely to exhibit greater intrinsic characteristics than men, whereas women in collectivistic cultures tend to exhibit greater interdependent characteristics than men in comparable cultures (Kashima et al. 1995). Safdar et al, (2008) compared dispositional traits and values in India, Pakistan, and the U.S., finding significant differences among participants from the three countries on measures of individualism-collectivism, gender role orientation, and emotional expressiveness. The social logics of face, honour, and respect, suggesting that these cultural orientations influence individual behaviour, social norms, and institutions. Understanding these cultural logics is crucial for promoting cross-cultural understanding and effective communication (Leung & Cohen, 2011).

Theatre of the Absurd and the Self-concept

Theatre of the Absurd, a theatrical movement that began in the mid of the twentieth century is a suitable heuristic means to understand the social representations of the person, specifically acculturated. This style of the theatrical event breaks away from the linear plot and presents characters as placed in a conflict, or a situation that symbolizes the existentialist notion and the quest for purpose. The latter themes stay most connected to the self's topic because they affect the individual's identity and their existence. The phenomenon of identity crisis is one of the prominent themes in the Theatre of the Absurd. Maybe most dramatically, three contemporary dramatists - Samuel Beckett, Eugène Ionesco, and Jean Genet - write about people who are lost in an existential drama and search for the meaning of their lives with no ostensible purpose. It must be said that such a portrayal can be compared to traditional cultural constructs of the self that is more often described through roles, goals, and expected functions.

Differences in self-identity are clearly seen by comparing existential anxiety of Theatre of the Absurd to collectivist cultures of the East which are characterized by understanding the self in the context of the community and social order. Linville and Fischer found that within many Asian focused societies the self-concept is more focused and stable due to the integration of family and societal roles into one's self-image. This is in contrast with the confusion of self-hood depicted in the Absurdist theatre, which can be explained by the fact that this form of art has emerged within the context of the 'Western' individualistic culture based on freedom and actualization. Thus, it is possible to consider that Theatre of the Absurd as a cultural critique of Western society based on the concerns of existentialism, identity, the meaning of life, and the collapse of the structures. The film forces the viewers to face the problem of the meaning of life and the existential nature of the individual's choice of own role. This is quite a thought-provoking challenge when applied to the cross-cultural experience as the concept of Self in the Absurd clashes with the collectivist/ holistic views of identity. Therefore, the Theatre of the Absurd offer a realistic and profound reflection of the essence of self that is quite distinguishable from the cultural perspectives of diversity. The latter characterizes the film in the representation of the fractured subjectivity that speculates on human life presenting the culture that forms the epistemology of the human individuality.

Indian Philosophical Perspectives on Identity and Existence

Indian culture and its thoughts regarding the self is well emerged in the Indian philosophy which embraces all the major forms of Indian philosophies. I Think the struggle for the self is core to Indian philosophy where Atman in Hinduism and Anatta in Buddhism is represented. These schools provide different perspectives toward the self and, therefore, depict a rich picture of it.

In Hindu philosophy, there are dualism views in which the entity of Atman is the real self of a person besides the body and mind. The Upanishads, two thousand and more years old treatise of the Hindus, define Atman as, everlasting, imperishable and same as Brahman, the Supreme Truth. This non-dualistic outlook is specifically articulated in Advaita Vedanta that proclaims the Liberating knowledge of identity between Atman and Brahman.

On the other hand, Nyāya-Vaiśeṣika school which is categorized as realism tradition of Indian philosophy propounds that the self is a 'real and individual substance which possesses cognition, desire and volition. It concerns the properties of separateness of self from other substances and subjectivity or the ability to have consciousness. Like

Mīmāṃsā, this school insists that the perceived continuity of consciousness requires a substratum hence its support for the self. There is a drastic shift of paradigm between the two religions, because while Christianity teaches that there is a self, Buddhism does not, or at least it postulates a different concept with the doctrine of no-self. This concept does not believe in the existence of the fixed and stable self. On the other hand, it regards the self as a set of complex processes and occurrences that are composite, shifting, and existentially empty. This attitude is also used to lessen suffering and attachment through the elimination of one's ego identity.

There is a degree of correlation between Indian philosophical thoughts and some of the Western concepts. For example, the Buddhist concept of no self is similar to Hume's bundle theory since these believe that there is no self, but a cluster of perceptions. Likewise, personal identity continuity of Nyāya-Vaiśeṣika corresponds with Locke's notion of the self that is unifying a person through memory and consciousness. Hence, the concept of self that is inherent in the Indian context present a pluralistic picture of existence and identity. This multileveled approach gives the possibility to give the work a sound foundation in metaphysical and psychological aspects and the detailed guidelines for the improvement of the life experience of individuals.

Impacts from Indian Cultural Factors

Cultural values such as family, religion, and spirituality greatly shape Self-concept among Indians. For instance, religiosity and spirituality are associated with self-worth among Indian adolescents. Gender differences are also significant, with Indian women often taught to prioritize the needs of their families and communities over their own, influencing their Self-concept. Traditional gender roles and expectations may limit opportunities for women, affecting their self-esteem. Regional differences within India also impact Self-concept. North Indian culture is generally more individualistic, while South Indian culture is more collectivistic, influencing how individuals in different parts of India view themselves and their societal roles.

The impact of globalization on Self-concept among Indians is another area of interest. As India becomes more integrated into the global economy and culture, changes in cultural values and norms may impact Self-concept . The caste system, a hierarchical social structure, can also affect Self-concept , with individuals from lower castes experiencing discrimination and marginalization, negatively affecting their self-esteem. Language and communication styles play a role in shaping Self-concept among Indians. For example, Hindi-speaking individuals may have a more interdependent Self-concept compared to English-speaking individuals. Education is another factor, with the emphasis on academic achievement and success in Indian culture leading to a more achievement-oriented Self-concept .

Generational differences also exist, with younger generations influenced more by global cultural values and norms, while older generations emphasize traditional cultural values and practices. Intersectionality, considering various cultural identities (e.g., religion, caste, gender, region), is important in examining the impact of culture on Self-concept among Indians.

The Enigma of Being: Exploring the Western Concept of Self

Western self-conception stands on a firm ground of philosophical, psychological, and neurological theorisations all painting a many-layered picture of the self. It is built on the foundation of critically analysing the works of the world's greatest philosophers and modern scientists, from psychology to neuroscience. For people of the western world self-concept is shaped with the help of philosophical, psycho logical and neuro-scientific concepts making a rather sophisticated perception of the self-idea along with the reference to the classical philosophical impulse, contemporary theories and the recent neuroscientific discoveries.

Philosophical Foundations

The discussion of the self as an object of philosophy in Western culture can be stated as pluralist and complex. Even in the rationalist tradition which emerged from philosophy of Descartes who said "Cogito, ergo sum" or "I think, therefore I exist", self is located at the core of rational cognition. This view also focuses on the aspect of individual autonomy. English philosopher John Locke combined the concept of personal identity and the continuity of consciousness claiming it to be based upon memory and experience. David Hume, however, disagreed with this argument claiming that in fact, self is just a collection of different perceptions that have no relation between themselves and that shift from one moment to another. Immanuel Kant later expanded the idea by coming with a distinction between the psychological self which is seen through the inner sense and experienced, and the transcendental self which is the self that lies beneath all the conscious experiences though cannot be experienced. Such a dualistic view raises questions about self-reflection and the limitations of people's thinking.

Psychological Perspectives

Looking at psychology there are several theories that have dictated the approach to the self. Freud's followers based their work on psychoanalytic theory which describes the human personality with reference to id, ego, and superego. The ego or rational self is the interpreter between the id and the superego which embodies the societal values. Building upon this, Carl Jung added the collective unconscious and archetypes into his theory, arguing for the There is an existence of common collective experiences and symbols that shape an individual's self. Cognitive and social theories of the contemporary psychology can also be included here. The concept of 'center of narrative gravity' developed by Daniel Dennett implies that people's identity forms according to the principles of narrative and integration of actual life events. Also, Patricia Churchland and her approach of eliminative materialism deny the actual existence of unified self, which uses this term as a part of folk science.

Neuroscientific Contributions

The scientific research in lifestyle pushed the question of the materiality of the self into the new directions. LZ noted that self-referential processing of information relates to the medial prefrontal cortex (mPFC) and the default mode network (DMN) that are implicated in self-reflection, self-observation, and other's perspective taking. These areas are related to what is termed as self-generated thought, which includes mind drifting attributed to day dreaming. Findings have shown the DMN to be more active when people are introspecting and thinking about themselves, which may point to the network's role in self-continuity. In addition, the communications of the DMN with other networks involving the CEN and the SN demonstrate the dynamic process of self-appraisal. For instance, the SN is useful in the identification of important stimuli as well as escalation of the same while the CEN aids in working memory and behavioral execution. It enables the individual to continuously adjust the level of functioning and meaning of personal identity as a result of internal and external conditions.

Self of the western tradition is a composition of philosophical musings, theories in psychology, and discoveries in neuroscience. It presents the self as an active and complex concept that depends on cognitive and social factors as well as on parts of the brain. This concept underlines the multilayered and multicultural nature of the self in the Western tradition as people enviously search for the mystery of the identity and consciousness.

Conclusion

Cultural influences in the development of Self-concept present a rich pattern of individual and shared aspects that mold people globally with regard to local and interpersonal factors. Finally, the independent and interdependent self-construct describe how cultural contexts shape the roles that individuals take within surrounding communities. In Western cultures, which are individualistic and emphasize personal accomplishments, self-identity is more oriented toward individual attributes. Whereas various cultures promote individualism, resulting in people crafting an identity for themselves and seeing themselves as unique entities, East Asian cultures, which aim to foster social order and welfare, press individuals into conforming to social roles.

The studies cited herein show that these cultural paradigms are not, in fact, impermeable: people of collectivistic cultures may pursue personal success, and those in individualistic cultures may be wedded to their relationships. The component of cultural collectivism and the aspect of emotional self-regulation also brought out other ways through which culture influences the construction of self. These differences of horizontal and vertical separation between collectivism and individualism provide further depth to the general themes, showing that how one is treated in a position of authority or peers can impact their identity.

This body of work points towards the value of cultural perspectives in regards to self-identity and necessitates understanding and appreciating cultural differences which are becoming more apparent due to globalization.

References

Atkin, R. (1981). The nature of self in primitive cultures.

Batey, Mark; Furnham, Adrian; Safiullina, Xeniya (2016) "Intelligence, General Knowledge and Self-esteem as Predictors of Creativity" Learning and Individual Differences, v20 n5 p532-535.

Best, E. (1982). Māori tradition and identity.

Chentsova-Dutton, Y. E., & Tsai, J. L. (2010). Self-focused attention and emotional reactivity: The role of culture. Journal of personality and social psychology, 98(3), 507-519

Choi, I., Nisbett, R. E., & Norenzayan, A. (1999). Causal attribution across cultures: Variation and universality. Psychological bulletin, 125(1), 47-63.

Dimkov, Petar. (2020). The concept of self in Eastern and Western philosophy. 197-204. 10.32591/coas.e-conf.05.17197d.

Doob, L. W. (1960). Becoming more civilized: A psychological exploration. Yale University Press.

Douglas, M. (1970). Natural symbols: Explorations in cosmology. Pantheon Books.

Garland, R., (2017). "The Measurement self-esteem and related constructs" Anu Arbai; Survey research centre,Institute for Social Research, pp. 45-158.

Hammershoj, Lars Geer (2009), "Creativity as a Question of Bildung", Journal of Philosophy of Education, v43 n4 p545-558.

Heine, S. J., Lehman, D. R., Markus, H. R., & Kitayama, S. (1999). Is there a universal need for positive self-regard? Psychological Review, 106(4), 766-794.

Heller, Kurt A. (2007), "Scientific Ability and Creativity" High Ability Studies, v18 n2 p209-234

Henner, T. (1998). Comparing EQ-I and TMMS scale scores. Unpublished manuscript.

Henry, Jim (2009) "Enhancing Creativity with M.U.S.I.C." Alberta Journal of Educational Research, v55 n2 p199-211.

Henshon, Suzanna E. (2011), "The Creative Path: An Interview with Dean Keith Simonton" Journal Articles; Roeper Review, v33 n2 p72-75.

Ivcevic, Zorana (2007), "Artistic and Everyday Creativity: An Act-Frequency Approach", Journal of Creative Behaviour, v41 n4 p271-290.

Kamarulzaman, Wirawani (2012), "Critical Review on Affect of Personality on Learning Styles' ' Online Submission, Paper presented at the International Conference on Arts, Social Science & Technology (2nd, Penang, Malaysia, Mar 3-5, 2012).

Kashima, Y., Yamaguchi, S., Kim, U., Choi, S.-C., Gelfand, M. J., & Yuki, M. (1995). Culture, gender, and self:

A perspective from individualism-collectivism research. Journal of Personality and Social Psychology, 69(5), 925-937.

Kathuria, R (2019). 'Self' in Indian Philosophy and Its parallel in Western Philosophy. International Journal of Indian Psychology, 7(1), 302-307,DIP:18.01.035/20190701, DOI:10.25215/0701.035

Kelson, W. (1943). The primitive mind and modern civilization. Routledge.

Kim, H. S., & Markus, H. R. (1999). Deviance or uniqueness, harmony or conformity? A cultural analysis. Journal of Personality and Social Psychology, 77(4), 785-800.

Kim, Kiwan; Karau, Steven J. (2018), "Working Environment and the Research Productivity of Doctoral Students in Management" Journal of Education for Business, v85 n2 p101-106.

Kirton, M. "Adaptors and Innovators: A description and Measure," Journal of Applied Psychology (61:5) 1976, pp 622-629.

Kizel, Arie (2012), "Cultivating Creativity and Self-Reflective Thinking through Dialogic Teacher Education" Online Submission, US-China Education Review A 2 p237-249.

Kolasa B.J. (1970). Introduction to Behavioural Science for Business. New Delhi: Wiley Eastern Private Limited.

La, Civita, Lori., (2003), An Examination of Emotional Intelligence Factors: Their relationship to Academic Achievement and the Implications for Retention of the At-Risk Community College student. Dissertation at Capella University.

Leung, K., & Cohen, D. (2011). Within- and between-culture variation: Individual differences and the cultural logics of honour, face, and dignity cultures. Journal of personality and social psychology, 100(3), 507-526.

Levy-Bruhl, L. (1927/1966). How natives think. Allen & Unwin.

Markus, H. R., & Kitayama, S. (1991). Culture and the self: Implications for cognition, emotion, and motivation. Psychological review, 98(2), 224-253.

Min-huei. Chien (2017), "An investigation of the relationship of organizational structure, Employee's personality and organizational citizenship behaviours". The journal of American Academy of business, Cambridge, Sep, 428-431.

Muhren and Amal (2018). "Factor affecting employees' motivation in Jordan," Dirasat, April, Vol. 17(2), pp. 7-23.

Oyserman, D., Coon, H. M., & Kemmelmeier, M. (2002). Rethinking individualism and collectivism: Evaluation of theoretical assumptions and meta-analyses. Psychological bulletin, 128(1), 3-72.

Pringle, Charles D.; DuBose, Philip B.; Yankey, Michael D. (2017), "Personality Characteristics and Choice of Academic Major: Are Traditional Stereotypes Obsolete" Journal Articles; College Student Journal, v44 n1 p131-142. psychology. New York: Academic Press.

Safdar, S., Friedlmeier, W., & Matsumoto, D. (2008). Geographical region and socialisation influences on dispositional traits and values in India, Pakistan, and the United States. Journal of Cross-Cultural Psychology, 39(3), 233-248.

Singelis, T. M. (1994). The measurement of independent and interdependent self-construal. Personality and social psychology bulletin, 20(5), 580-591.

Storme, Martin; Lubart, Todd (2017), "Conceptions of Creativity and Relations with Judges' Intelligence and Self-esteem". New York: Basic Books.

Triandis, H. C. (1995). Individualism and collectivism. Westview Press.

CHAPTER THREE

Bridging Worlds: Traditionalism, Ethnocentrism, and Multiculturalism

- **Adithi Priyadarshini Prabhu**

Background

Knowledge is information with a purpose or application. Cross-cultural psychology can be described as the study of how different cultures have influenced people's minds. Any cross-cultural psychology study must use at least two samples that are representative of at least two different cultural groups to draw findings. The study of cross-cultural psychology looks at psychological variation and the underlying causes of it. Cross-cultural psychology examines traits and behaviour among many cultural groups with a focus on both variance and human universals. Although it has been said that cultural psychology is focused primarily on psychological processes inside a particular culture, comparison is still an element of it. Gaining an understanding of the cross-cultural dimensions of knowledge is essential to establishing global connections. Three essential components of cross-cultural psychology are traditionalism, ethnocentrism, and multiculturalism. By gaining an understanding of them, we may better negotiate the subtleties and complexity of cross-cultural encounters, cultivating empathy and advancing an inclusive global society.

Traditionalism is defined as respecting and upholding one's own social group's traditions, morality, and standards. It also involves openly opposing any change to deeply ingrained principles, customs, or traditions. Traditionalism is sometimes defined as the preservation and advancement of the culture and practice unique to past civilizations, not all of which are limited to those that have thrived economically, aesthetically, and philosophically. Ethnocentrism fosters prejudice by using one's own culture as the yardstick for judging other civilizations. It occurs when a person believes that their cultural group is superior to another. In a manner, ethnocentrism is exaggerated. Because of the massive size of the dominant and the fact that its people occupy the majority of positions of power, values and standards embraced by any significant number have a great deal of influence. The idea that different cultural groups have the right to pursue their particular developmental paths and to have their particular activities, values, and norms is promoted by the individual's psychological and theoretical perspective known as multiculturalism. Multiculturalism not only supports the understanding of unity for all national and cultural groups. The core of the multicultural perspective is self-discovery, which results in self-awareness. The social structure is not uniform, diverse identities and cultures coexist, and differences are not seen as sources of conflict but as sources of richness in multiculturalism, which enables transformation in society (Banks & Banks, 2010; Parekh, 2000).

Traditionalism

Traditionalism does not have a single description that applies to all instances, and it is challenging to identify one that captures the essence of traditionalism's most important characteristics. According to some authors, traditionalism is the extent to which people adhere to cultural ideals, traditions, and customs (Salari, Shiu, and Zhang, 2017). While this definition can capture the relationship between traditionalism and the intensity of expression of such a commitment, the actual distinction between traditionalism and non-traditionalism is not made explicit in this definition. According to Shils (1958), traditionalism is the intentional, deliberate embrace of traditional norms while fully cognizant of their traditional origins and claiming that their quality is derived from that transmission. This definition is useful since it identifies sacredness as one of the essential elements; nevertheless, the inclusion of self-consciousness can also be disputed. Traditional culture restricts people's choices and controls their lives. The majority of their daily activities are assigned to them by authorities, leaving little possibility for change. Traditional civilizations dictate individuals' perceptions of good and evil, pleasant and unpleasant objects, worthwhile and useless activities, and sanity and insanity through religious as well as other cultural imperatives. According to traditionalism, the cultural movements of the 20th century persisted as a long-term subversive agenda in the West and some countries in East Asia, rather than coming to an end or starting with the Soviet Union or Communist China. The Frankfurt School

Diaspora, the CIA, and a variety of pathological progressives are important groups involved. It would be incorrect to attribute this cultural shift to a particular group. However, it is noteworthy that only certain groups are disproportionately overrepresented in the upkeep of these principles. The fight over tradition is nothing new; such principles date back to the Protestant Reformation and the Age of Enlightenment (Logos Times, 2021). Traditionalism requires the capacity to see how a thriving civilization is deteriorating. A traditionalist must understand that advancement is not always the end-all and be-all. A more equal, "peaceful," and bountiful society may have resulted from Enlightenment liberalism as well as industrialization, yet these developments essentially go against the standards of old civilization. Traditionalism essentially rejects the Whig view of history, which holds that humanity was imprisoned in superstitious ignorance for ages before emerging around the Renaissance and progressing toward ever-greater freedom and understanding. According to the Traditionalist, it wouldn't be weird to read Medieval thinkers and determine that they were accurate while their predecessors in the so-called "Enlightenment" were mistaken. Traditionalism contends that trait openness, a component of Western civilization's enlightenment that runs directly counter to Christian and/or Indo-European morality, is one of humanity's downfalls. Fewer scientific discoveries were made during the Qing Dynasty because of the East's resistance to change, but this effectively kept Eastern civilization from being culturally impacted by progressive ideas (to a certain extent). As a result, the East frequently sees the decline of Western civilization as a direct result of progressive ideology. The essential tenet of traditionalism is that knowledgeable and immutable reality, which includes morality, exists. Although the Middle Ages were not always correct, they were also not always wrong. And if the "Enlightenment" folks weren't always correct, they weren't always wrong either. On the identical principles, they are both demonstrated to be true or false. Traditionalism is not purely individualistic or collectivist.

Traditionalism emphasises individual responsibility, but moral standards must be actively upheld by the community as a whole. The relevance of communal (duty-based) morality above individualistic moral relativism is held by traditionalists. Traditionalism can be characterized metaphysically as a workable "meta-analysis" of long-standing customs, religious texts, or spiritual teachings that have formed the foundation of great civilizations in both the East and the West. recognizing the folklore, morality, prophecies, and eschatology that are included therein as being identical. Traditionalists can now comprehend the descriptive and normative foundations for the idea behind the aforementioned commonalities. According to psychologist Barry Schwartz (2004), people in today's consumption-driven societies spend far too much time selecting different foods, furnishings, automobiles, clothes, collective investment schemes, and vacation spots. This abundance of choices can result in "choice congestion" and dissatisfaction over errors people make when using their choices. Focusing on traditionalism and psychology, it is thought to have had a significant impact on the creation of new psychological theories, particularly Transpersonal psychology. Transpersonal psychology is a mode of thought that takes into account several factors that the schools of psychology previously ignored. Transpersonal authors aimed to promote mystical experiences and transformed states of consciousness as useful instruments for realizing people's potential. Here, the term "transpersonal" is used to refer to something that transcends the self. Therefore, according to transpersonal psychologists, the only way to achieve psychical healing is to let go of the self which is thought to be a source of restriction to obtain access to an esoteric reality that is eternally relevant. Individuals may eventually be able to get over "negative" emotions like guilt or anxiety because of this state. Because it strives to overcome the limits that transpersonal psychologists see in the so-called first force (Freudian philosophy), second force (behaviourist school), and third force, transpersonal psychology is sometimes known as the "fourth force" (humanist approach). It yearns to imagine a levelling human mentality to build a radical new viewpoint. Accordingly, it believes that behavioural and psychoanalytical Freudian thought have both attempted to address the lower levels of this scale, that is the transpersonal belongs to the transcendental, but have fallen short of doing so. The writings of Greek-Armenian Traditionalist George Ivanovich Gurdjieff (1877–1949), particularly his emphasis on the necessity of spiritual awakening and his theorization of the idea of "The Fourth Way," have been particularly influential for the transpersonal movement. William James (1842–1910) and Carl Gustav Jung (1875–1961) are two of the most notable forerunners of the Transpersonal School of Psychology. Transpersonal psychology has seen a sharp rise in popularity since the 1970s when concepts of spiritual development began to transcend the confines of psychology. More secularly oriented psychology sectors have criticized transpersonal psychology harshly for incorporating perennialism or traditionalism into psychology (Diaz, 2010). Traditionalism and modernization do not go hand-in-hand. Traditionalism tends to delay modernization, disrupt peaceful interpersonal interactions, and place restrictions on individualism and independence. The first problem is that traditionalism hinders and delays the modernisation and growth of communities and perhaps even entire nations. This is a very severe problem since it influences communities' futures and decides how successful the community will be. Individuals would continue to develop and adapt as our environment changes, just like all other animals. As a result, we have been able to eradicate numerous diseases, extend life expectancy, and instantaneously access knowledge. However, some individuals reject modernization and choose to live in ways that put themselves in danger and impede the social and economic progress of their countries. Before the Renaissance period, religion and culture restrained the advancement of science during the 'Dark Ages'. The state of civilization today could be far more advanced were it not for this oppression. Millions of lives have been saved by vaccinations, which are regarded as being one of the important innovations in contemporary history. Traditionalists continue to oppose childhood immunisation despite overwhelming consensus among scientists and other professional organisations. These traditionalists reject research from institutions such as 'The World Health Organization that refutes myths like the idea that vaccinations cause autism or that they overtax the immune system. The number of parents who refuse to vaccinate their children is rising, and this problem is getting more critical as a result. These parents endanger not just their children but also the community. Another illustration would be the opposition to rural communities' industrialization and modernization. The industrialization of rural areas has various advantages, including improved education and employment rates. Traditionalists, on the other hand, oppose the modernisation of these villages because they claim that it will ruin their culture. Traditionalists are slowing down the rate at which the rural population is vanishing. As was previously noted, industrialization improves economic opportunities and affluence, which have a favourable impact on health and quality of life. This has a detrimental impact on their community. However, there is evidence demonstrating how individuals and communities continue to uphold their culture and customs despite modernization and advancement, negating the traditionalists' argument. Tradition and heritage are not necessarily lost in the name of development. Traditionalism also causes a split in the peaceful exchange and coexistence of people, which is another problem. There is a virtual barrier that prevents engagement, acceptance, and equal opportunity amongst individuals from different cultures and ethnicities, which is difficult to acknowledge. Communities' ability to develop and evolve is badly impacted by this. This cultural barrier separates people and is the cause of innumerable debates, conflicts, and even battles that have destroyed or rendered unrecoverable communities and cultures. However, each of these problems does have a solution and a course of action, some of which are not too difficult. To address the problem of traditionalism stifling modernisation, governments should first direct their financial resources toward modernising rural communities' agricultural businesses, as well as toward improving infrastructure and education. Governments should openly denounce such false views and make vaccinations mandatory in the case of traditionalists who think immunizations are harmful. Last but not least, customs that violate people's human rights and are inhumane should be outright prohibited and subject to severe penalties to discourage further use.

Ethnocentrism

Coming into the light of ethnocentrism, Sumner (1906) first introduced the term ethnocentrism to describe the propensity to see other groups through the lens of one's group. However, Charles Darwin (1874) noticed ethnocentric behaviour in tribes. He noticed how tribes showed greater sympathy for their own than for other groups. This propensity may be a universal trait of intercultural relationships (LeVine & Campbell, 1972). Sumner's concise but in-depth and thorough analysis of ethnocentrism in Folk traditions is still the key source of theory on the topic. Although Coser (1956) referenced Marx and other previous theorists for some elements of ethnocentrism, Sumner may have coined the terms "ethnocentrism" and "ingroup" and was responsible for giving it broad consequences for the social sciences. Sumner also acknowledged prior findings by Ludwig Gumplowicz. Sumner's significant passage served as a point of reference for later social theories and models on conflict, ethnic connections, and intergroup disputes and attitudes. Social scientists who researched on the same grounds as Sumner found most of the same occurrences in their studies.

Ethnocentrism is mostly not a characteristic of cross-cultural psychology, though, as each different phenomenon is seen in its context and no evaluative posture is taken toward differences. Numerous academics have argued for this position in the fields of psychology and anthropology

(Herskovits, 1948). Throughout human history, ethnocentrism has persisted in almost all cultures. One must be aware of individuals outside of one's country or cultural limits to feel morally and intellectually superior. Knowing enough about others to consider their way of life inferior to one's own is another requirement for feeling superior to other people. Therefore, interaction with the outside world is required for ethnocentrism to establish itself and grow. Keith, D. (2019) in his book on Cross-Cultural Psychology thinks ethnocentrism to be a characteristic of all people. The author suggested that ethnocentrism can manifest itself in a variety of ways, including with or without animosity against other groups, but it's always characterised by the propensity to exalt one's group (the ingroup). Despite the possibility that ethnocentrism has evolutionary roots, a range of psychological characteristics and disorders have been linked to it. Although research has suggested a link between ethnocentrism and authoritarian rule as well as between ethnocentrism and fundamentalism, studies examining these psychological characteristics have typically been correlational or have lacked the necessary experimental controls to allow causal inferences. Researchers in the modern era have looked into ethnocentrism in a variety of contexts, such as religious practice (Banyasz, Tokar, & Kaut, 2014), purchasing preferences (Guo & Zhou, 2017), and perceptions of immigrants (Banks, 2016). In a study of three types of group selfishness (ethnocentrism, fundamentalism, and anthropocentrism) involving Australian university students, Bizumic and Duckitt (2007) discovered that people who strongly support their human groups over others also frequently support humans over other species. Therefore, discrimination against animals was linked to a lack of empathy for other human outgroups. However, ethnocentrism did not link with negative attitudes toward relevant outgroups in general, unlike other forms of self-centeredness. Furthermore, although Raden (2003) found some subgroups of a large probability sample of white Americans to exhibit classic (Sumnerian) ethnocentrism (i.e., positive perceptions toward the in-group, hostility toward the out-group), in-group bias (without the implication of unfavourable views of out-groups) was more common in his sample. The difference between the basic way of ethnocentrism and more prevalent in-group bias, which Raden suggested may be a halfway between both the extremes of traditional ethnocentrism and the lack of ethnocentrism, is important methodologically as a result of this discovery.

Bizumic and Duckitt (2012) pointed out that ethnocentrism goes beyond outgroup negativity and ingroup positivity in their attempt to define what it is and is not. Such recent research suggests that ethnocentrism is more common than the Sumerian perspective might imply and that it takes many different forms. Although an ethnocentric judgement contains an emotional component as well, it can be thought of as a cognitive phenomenon. It is typically referred to as an ethnic stereotype in its cultural form. The fundamental human propensity for ethnocentrism has been extensively studied by writers (for example, LeVine & Campbell, 1972; Neuliep, Hintz, & McCroskey, 2005; Shuya, 2007). Ethnocentrism has also shown itself in how people view the intercultural ability and beauty of people from various cultures (Neuliep et al., 2005). In addition to the individual and intergroup levels, ethnocentric prejudice also affects scientists who research psychological phenomena across cultural boundaries (e.g.,

Berry et al., 2002; Hofstede, 2007). Several authors, including Campbell (1970), have suggested research techniques meant to lessen the contaminating effect of ethnocentrism in social scientific inquiries. As a process of enculturating youngsters into a society, ethnocentrism may appear to be "automatic" (LeBaron, 2003); others regard it almost as a tabula rasa process in which the infant learns the culture and attitudes of the society (LeVine, 1982). On the other hand, other authors have maintained that ethnocentrism has an evolutionary basis. For instance, Wilson (1978) presented the concept that ethnocentric tribal groupings might benefit biologically from aggressiveness as well as other related behaviours. Wilson claimed that while individual behaviours (such as particular types of violence) may not be passed down genetically, the cultural institutions that sustain them may have been. Therefore, adaptable groups were those who were effective in creating a "us" and "them" division in the world. Similar to this, Thayer (2004) advanced the idea that individuals have an affection for those to whom they are biologically linked. According to this theory, people should be expected to support their immediate family first, followed by additional relatives, their ethnicity, and lastly others. This viewpoint, according to Thayer, acknowledges the natural tendency to prioritize those who are biologically related, though it does not imply that ethnocentrism is not affected by environmental factors (such as culture, religion, and political beliefs). Furthermore, there is some evidence to indicate that an ethnically pure culture (in which people might be presumed to be more biologically similar) may demonstrate higher levels of ethnocentrism over a more diversified one (Neuliep, Chaudoir, & McCroskey, 2001).

Ross (1991) argued in favour of the idea of something like a cultural evolutionary program in place of the imperfect sociobiological explanation for ethnocentrism. In his discussion of the connection between heredity and human nature, Simon (1980) listed many cultural universals and opined that there is insufficient evidence to draw a firm conclusion on whether or not they are founded on genetics.

Cross-cultural research can be impacted by ethnocentrism on three different levels: the introduction of culturally unique meaning, the selection of research areas, and the development of ideas. It can cause a loss of societal relevance and inaccurate judgments of other people's actions. Cultural biases can also impair theory-driven research. Cross-cultural psychology seeks to lessen the ethnocentrism of psychology in one significant way: by acknowledging the gaps in our current understanding (the first goal) and attempting to expand our data and theory by incorporating many cultures (the second and third goals), we can lessen the discipline's reliance on one particular culture. We run the risk of increasing ethnocentrism by pursuing this goal of eliminating it because it entails gathering and analyzing evidence from various cultures. Generally speaking, the likelihood of negative assessments of the difference increases with the degree of the cultural or behavioural difference. Numerous psychological factors that seem to be connected to the behaviours we refer to as ethnocentrism have been researched by scientists. Narcissism, religious fanaticism, significant personal characteristics, intolerance for uncertainty, and authoritarianism are a few of them. Researchers discovered several connections between ethnocentrism and traits that fall along a continuum of "open- mindedness." The researchers hypothesized that narcissism may predispose people to have ethnocentric attitudes after discovering a positive connection between narcissism (self-centeredness) and intergroup ethnocentrism in a group of university students in New Zealand. When researching Canadian students, Altemeyer (2003) discovered strong connections between religious ethnocentrism, Manitoban ethnocentrism, and religious ethnocentrism. Siegman (1958) investigated how cultural influences affected the relationship between ethnocentrism neuroticism and intelligence (Keith, 2019), concluding that the relationship between ethnocentrism and the two personal traits (neuroticism and intelligence) may be lessened in the context of a culture that supports ethnocentric attitudes. The implication of this finding would seem to be (unsurprisingly) that a supportive cultural background is a significant factor in individuation. Most recently, Cargile (2013) discovered that ambiguity tolerance (but not cultural knowledge) decreased ethnocentrism in students; those who were less able to accept ambiguity tended to be more ethnocentric. Researchers have examined parental traits and parenting approaches in this context because parents, naturally, play a significant role in how ethnocentrism develops in children. Numerous research has demonstrated a link between parental traits and actions and children's ethnocentrism. Children who had parents with somewhat harsh disciplinary methods were much more likely to have ethnocentric attitudes (Epstein and Komorita, 1966). Through research on Midwestern American students and their mothers, Mosher and Scodel (1960) discovered a correlation between the children's ethnocentrism and that of their mothers, but not between the mothers' authoritarianism. Even in less developed nations, studies are still sparse in number and haven't made much of an impression of psychology as a science. In other words, the level of scientific colonization in psychology is fairly significant, though difficult to assess and even harder to correct.

Multiculturalism

The idea that people from different cultural backgrounds have the right to pursue their particular developmental paths and to have their particular activities, values, and norms is promoted by the individual's psychological and theoretical perspective known as Multiculturalism. Multiculturalism not only supports the acknowledgement of inclusivity for all national and cultural groups. The core of the multicultural perspective is self-discovery, which results in self-awareness. A psychologist using a multicultural approach must make more connections with different groups and research their ideas, traditions, and lifestyles. By offering evidence regarding the behaviour, motivation, and expression of people who live in various national, ethnic, and cultural contexts, cross-cultural psychology, utilizing a multicultural approach, enhances national schools of psychology. Although it can also be acquired through other sustained immersive experiences, multiculturalism is common among immigrants and their offspring (Berry, 1997; Martin & Shao, 2016; Padilla, 2006). The fundamental question, "What makes someone multicultural?" has been addressed in a variety of ways over the past 30 years by the fields of management, psychology, market research, sociology, and anthropology. These responses have been grouped into five themes: the background, the acculturation process, knowledge and skills, cognitions, and identification. Determining individual-level diversity by contextual elements, such as historical experience, environment, cultural heritage, interpersonal ties, and national policy, is a minor but persistent theme throughout disciplines and over time. In a multicultural nation, a variety of circumstances, including political, economic, and other situational repercussions, may make it difficult for many ethnic groups to coexist peacefully. It is frequently believed that everyone with heritage from more than just one cultural community, or from a group that is different from the majority culture, is multicultural. Other scholars concentrate on the sociological context of interpersonal interactions that can compel, encourage, or discourage people from adhering to particular cultural affinities. For instance, sociological and anthropological research examines how social networks and interactions may cause multiracial people to gravitate toward or away from their small cultural groups, particularly for those with less authority or status or whose ethnic ancestry is different from the majority in a society. It has been demonstrated that a confluence of socio-political variables, including societal attitudes toward minorities, national immigration policy, and the degree of cultural variety in a region, affects multiculturalism on an individual level. Such context-based conceptualizations are advantageous in that they explicitly acknowledge how geography, traditional culture, governance, history, and interpersonal relationships, which are mostly external-based elements, both direct and restrain people's multiculturalism. All other conceptualizations primarily ignore these contextual factors. Psychological acculturation is the term used to describe how an individual's culture transforms as a result of ongoing, direct international encounters (Ward & Geeraert, 2016). Focus on the concept in this tradition highlights the sequential process of cultural adaptation, frequently following migration, and typically distinguishing between the person's heritage culture and the host, adopted, or main culture (Berry, 1997). Research on people becoming multicultural in different ways is hampered by the definition of multiculturalism also as a psychological phenomenon of gradually adopting another culture. People frequently become multicultural, for instance, through simultaneous absorption in other cultures (Martin & Shao, 2016). The conventional idea of acculturation is not adaptable enough to take into account multiple routes to multiculturalism as well as the varieties of multiculturalism that come from them.

One of psychology's newest and most vibrant subfields, multicultural psychology has been recognised as essential to comprehending how culture functions in psychological research. The study of racial and ethnic minority concerns in psychology has developed over the past 30 years to the point where it can now be viewed as a substantial and active specialization in the framework of American psychology. After the well-developed behavioural and psychodynamic theories and the humanistic perspective on psychology, multicultural psychology is typically described as the "fourth force" in psychological studies (Hall, 2009). It is crucial to comprehend its historical development. The culture and the discipline of psychology have benefited greatly from multicultural psychology. Therefore, we can say that multicultural psychology is a rapidly evolving field that is changing the way we view cultural variety, especially when it comes to studying human behaviours. Understanding the cultural variances in numerous facets of day-to-day life experiences is the primary focus of this field. The many mental processes, acceptable and inappropriate behaviours, and "normal" and "abnormal" behaviour orientations in daily life are just a few of them. The study of multicultural psychology has aided in identifying an individual within many cultures and promoting communication between people from various cultural backgrounds. There are a few challenges concerning multiculturalism. We should avoid attempting to comprehend multiculturalism in one of these circumstances via the lens of the other. Each nation has a unique demographic mix and distribution, as well as distinct migration histories and intergroup connections within a multicultural setting. Of course, it is crucial to link the unique multicultural experiences to how issues of variation and change are viewed within the national framework of society. Recognizing that relationships between groups and individuals within any multicultural setting are prone to change and development is crucial since multiculturalism is a process. This might go either way; a climate of amicable and courteous interactions between various groups might not persist eternally. Peaceful coexistence may be manipulated or violently interrupted. No society in the modern globalised world is homogeneous, thus every society has elements of diversity and distinction. In addition to cultural and religious variations, other aspects of social variety may have an equal impact. Additionally, there is a great deal of overlap between cultural and religious variety and other social divisions, notably those related to money and politics. Effective management of these disparities is required, and in particular, respect for diversity must be linked with the building of a feeling of shared ground among the differences. Otherwise, there is a risk that diversity- related tensions will worsen, especially in light of ongoing discussions and attitudes in society. Differentiation can be politicized in a variety of ways, especially during periods of fast social upheaval, economic hardship, or political disaster. Numerous instances of minority ethnic groups being demonized and "blamed" for social issues by the dominant culture can be found throughout history. Another of the issues of multiculturalism seems to be to make sure that any cross-cultural conflict inside society is controllable while still ensuring the implementation of social equality and protection to all sectors of the society. Multiculturalism does not necessarily aim to prevent such conflict.

Conclusion

Traditionalism is the emphasis on one's own group's past, frequently linking it to more significant organizations like cultural, regional, national, and religious ones. It can also be used to describe social and economic conservatism when people prioritize maintaining societal norms, beliefs, and practices. By adopting one's culture as the standard to evaluate other civilizations, ethnocentrism breeds prejudice. It is not specific to any one culture and can happen to anyone in most cultures and societies. Ethnocentrism in psychology might make findings less generalizable since the researchers might not have considered cultural variety. Despite the possibility that ethnocentrism has evolutionary roots, a variety of psychological characteristics and disorders have been linked to it. Although research has suggested a link between ethnocentrism and authoritarian rule as well as between ethnocentrism and fundamentalism, studies examining these psychological characteristics have typically been correlational or have lacked the necessary experimental control systems to allow causal inferences. Despite the possibility that ethnocentrism has evolutionary roots, a variety of psychological characteristics and disorders have been linked to it. Although research has suggested a link between ethnocentrism and authoritarian rule as well as between ethnocentrism and fundamentalism, studies examining these psychological characteristics have typically been correlational or have lacked the necessary experimental control systems to allow causal inferences. The idea of multiculturalism is sometimes perceived as a means of distancing diverse societies and states from their cultural ties. This does not imply, however, that countries with a single dominant culture are the most just; rather, it suggests that multiculturalism should indeed be incorporated into a state's public life in a variety of ways. This could result in a new type of public culture that encourages involvement with and respect for diversity while also valuing the cultures that people live within and between.

References

Breitenbeck, D. (2019, February 27). A summary of traditionalism. The Everyman. https://everymancommentary.com/a-brief-summary-of-traditionalism/

Diaz, M. D. (2010, January 1). Traditionalism. Encyclopedia of Psychology and Religion. https://www.academia.edu/94619449/Traditionalism

Guy-Evans, O. (2023, February 16). What is ethnocentrism and how does it impact psychological research? Study Guides for Psychology Students - Simply Psychology. https://simplypsychology.org/ethnocentrism.html

IvyPanda. (2018, May 18). Multicultural Psychology as a Subspecialty of Psychology. https://ivypanda.com/essays/multicultural-psychology/

John W. Berry, Ype H. Poortings, Marshall H. Segall, Pierre R. Dasen (2002). Cross-Cultural Psychology: Research and Applications, (Second Edition). Cambridge University Press, New York

Keith, D. (2019). Cross-Cultural Psychology: Contemporary Themes and Perspectives, (Second Edition). John Wiley & Sons Ltd

LeVine, R. A. (2001). Ethnocentrism. International Encyclopedia of the Social & Behavioral Sciences, 4852–4854. doi:10.1016/b0-08-043076-7/00857-0033fvbnm,./

n.a. (2020, February 11). Harmful effect of Traditionalism on Modernization & Development: Free Essay Example, 1902 words. Samplius. https://samplius.com/free-essay-examples/harmful-effect-of-traditionalism-on-modernization-development/

n.a. (2021, January 8). What is traditionalism? The Logos Times | A Traditionalist Perspective. https://logostimes.sites.icbix.com/2021/01/08/what-is-traditionalism/

n.a. (2023, February 15). Multiculturalism research paper. iResearchNet. https://www.iresearchnet.com/research-paper-examples/culture-research-paper/multiculturalism-research-paper/

Nye, M. (2007, July 20). (PDF) the challenges of multiculturalism - researchgate. ResearchGate. https://www.researchgate.net/publication/263889929_The_Challenges_of_Multicultur alism

Vora, D., Martin, L., Fitzsimmons, S. R., Pekerti, A. A., C, L., & Raheem, S. (2018, December). Multiculturalism within individuals: A review, critique, and agenda for ... ResearchGate. https://www.researchgate.net/publication/329457499_Multiculturalism_within_indivi

duals_A_review_critique_and_agenda_for_future_research

Yılmaz, F. (2016, May 13). Multiculturalism and multicultural education: A case study of teacher candidates' perceptions. Taylor & Francis. https://www.tandfonline.com/doi/full/10.1080/2331186X.2016.1172394\

CHAPTER FOUR

Ramayana: A Tapestry of Cultural Interpretations

- Ayushi Kadam

Background

India as we know, Bharat is seen to house a multitude of cultures, and with these cultures there come novel and advanced interpretations of symbols, traditions, practices, and scriptures. This is especially seen now because the country is moving towards modernization and globalization. We get to see many similarities and dissimilarities that have been preexisting in India for a very long time. One such example is the great epic written by the great poet of India, Valmiki, is the Ramayana which is also known as the Valmiki Ramayana. In this epic, Valmiki writes about the struggles, victories, and the many close-knit relationships of the protagonist. It is known through this very epic that Lord Rama travels from his birthplace, Ayodhya after he is exiled because his father promised his stepmother, all the way to Sri Lanka to rescue his wife, Sita Ma. Hence, the influence of this particular scripture is seen throughout India. While that is true, the influence of this epic isn't only restricted to India. Places like Sri Lanka and Cambodia have also been influenced as the temples of Lord Rama can be seen there as well. This is one of the main reasons why there might be different versions of stories or parts of the stories of this very epic in different regions of India. This is why the study aims to understand these variations and differences in the stories as well as the interpretations of this epic. This study would help us better understand the different values, rituals, and practices of a culture that will be revealed. It also lets us know about the ethnogeography and the ethnobotany of the particular culture. For example, we know Hanuman travels to Dronagiri mountain to get the Sanjeevni herb which is only found in that area, and carries the mountain as a whole, while doing so pieces of this mountain fell in certain places and now it is found in those places. We know that the practices of a culture are influenced by the resources available in the area and the geography. So, it is important to know how much variation exists between these cultures in one country to better understand the psyche of the people of that region and their reception towards their traditions and culture. This also will help give a deeper understanding of how the stories were passed on to the newer generations as the study delves into those aspects.

A Tapestry of Cultural Interpretations

Homo sapiens are the only species on earth to divide themselves based on "culture." Humans define culture for themselves through their beliefs, values, geography, customs, etc. Tylor made it very obvious in Anthropology (1881) that only man possesses culture as that term is understood. For around 50 years, anthropologists did well with this understanding of culture. As anthropological science developed, more introspection on the nature of its subject matter and concepts resulted in a proliferation and variety of definitions of culture. American anthropologists A.L. Kroeber and Clyde Kluckhohn cited 164 definitions of culture in their book Culture: A Critical Review of Concepts and Definitions (1952). These definitions included "learned behavior," "ideas in the mind," "a logical construct," "a statistical fiction," "a psychic defense mechanism," and more. Kroeber and Kluckhohn, as well as a large number of other anthropologists, favor the definition—or conception—that culture is an abstraction, or more specifically, "an abstraction from behavior." (White. A. L, n.d.). The APA defines culture as:

1. The distinctive customs, values, beliefs, knowledge, art, and language of a society or a community. These values and concepts are passed on from generation to generation, and they are the basis for everyday behaviors and practices.
2. The characteristic attitudes and behaviors of a particular group within society, such as a profession, social class, or age group.

The Ramayana or Rama's Journey is one of the epic poems of India. It was originally written in Sanskrit by the great poet and sage Valmiki and has 24,000 couplets distributed in 7 books (Bala Kanda, Ayodhya Kanda, Aranya Kanda, Kishkindha Kanda, Sundara Kanda, Yuddha Kanda, Uttara Kanda). The poem talks about Lord Rama, who was the oldest son of King Dashratha. Rama ends up marrying the daughter of Lord Janaka after winning a contest set by him. he was then banished into exile for 14 years by his father because of the promise he made with his other wife Kaikye. As Rama, Sita, and Lakshman venture into the forest, they meet Shurpanaka who has fallen in love with Lakshman but he denies her affection she proceeds to force him but he slices her nose. After this, we can see that she goes to her brother Ravana and from then, he decides to get revenge for his beloved sister and hence ends up dressing as a sage and venturing into the forest with the intention of kidnapping Sita which he succeeds in. we then see Rama travel to Lanka to save Sita from Ravana's clutches. The main message taught to children while we were told about the Ramayana is that good always wins over evil or good prevails. Each character in this epic has their own story and their own characteristics and represents different perspectives as well. Rama represents qualities like brave, loyal, and dutiful, then comes Lakshman represents brotherhood, and brave, Sita represents purity, innocence, and motherhood, Kaikey represents greed, motherhood, etc. there are many more characters with different characteristics and different psyches.

The Ramayana has many psychological aspects at play. Firstly, the great interpersonal relationships among the brothers in seen when Bharatha decides to deny his position as king because he knew that his older brother was the rightful heir and then it is seen even between Lakshman and Rama when he insists on joining him and Sita into exile. It is also seen between Rama and Hanuman as well. A lot of times because of new fantasy and romantic literature many people view Lakshman as the sidekick but throughout the epic, he is seen as more than just that as also emphasized by the poet when he writes lines like "sahalakshmana" or "sahasaumitri" which means with Lakshman. The Ramayana is seen to have multiple heroes and both the brothers were a heroic pair (Goldman. R, 1980).

Gender has slowly become more talked about since it does not only relate to biological factors now, but the individual's psyche or psychology also matters just as much. In Indian culture, women are seen to have less caliber and competencies. In a study done on gender manifestations and implications of Sita in Ramayana, the study saw that women were put into the role of more feminine and submissive roles by male chauvinists since Ramayana (Balamurali. E, Hariharasudan. A, 2021).

During the lockdown, the legendary series of the Ramayana is crucial. In the Ramayana, there is an event where Sita in Ramayana teaches us the value of not crossing our own Lakshman Rekha, which is our front door because she did so and caused difficulties for herself in a manner similar to others who do the same. SOP (standard operating procedure) These events, which were planned in recent days with the goal of praising and recognizing the efforts of health and security personnel, may have had a significant impact on people's way of life by successfully persuading the populace based on their culture and religious beliefs to view the lockdown period favorably (Tripathi. A, Pandey. S, Tiwari. P, 2020).

It demonstrates how psychological ownership may be more significant than actual participation. The term "psychological ownership" describes the sensation that something is "my" (Alok and Israel, 2012; Pierce, Kostova, and Dirks, 2001: Van Dyne and Pierce, 2004). Sugriva confronted Rama because he felt strongly about the issue and cared about Rama's welfare. Before addressing what, they needed to say, each advisor brought up these points. It was more of an obligation to protect what they saw as their own than a strong desire to influence decisions. It is important to conduct empirical research on how psychological ownership and involvement interact (Alok. K, 2014).

In order to sustain a person's welfare, psychological, philosophical, and spiritual traditions have placed emphasis on the quality of consciousness. To improve well-being, a person also needs a prescribed nutrition supply in their environment. According to the classical idea of well-being, there are two major categories of well-being: hedonic well-being, which is connected to the. The difference between happiness and eudaimonic well-being has to do with human potential According to a different idea of well-being, a person will contribute to well-being if they live in accordance with their daimon or actual selves. Happiness is a result of realizing one's actual essence, which is regarded as the eudaimonic concept of wellness (hedonic well-being). Individuals who frequently engage in immoral, malevolent, and covert behavior will experience mental and bodily problems. All of these psychological wellness tenets were contrasted with the Ramayana and Mahabharata, two Hindu epics (Panguluri. P, 2018).

Ramayana has multiple psychotherapy techniques to help with intense negative emotions like anger, lust, sadness, and fear. For example, when Lakshman expresses anger when Bharatha comes to see Rama and Lakshmana assumes he is here for war. Rama uses a technique similar to perspective-taking and reviewing alternate views from cognitive therapy. He does this by asking Lakshmana to not jump to conclusions and hear his brother out first. The next example is when Ravana's uncle Mareecha counsels Ravana that lusting behind Sita would only bring destruction and that it is sin to lust behind another woman and also his brother Vibhishana does the same by telling him to give up on his desire for Sita and let her go. The technique used is supportive therapy and telling him to distance himself from Sita (Bhide. S, Kurhade. C, Jagannathan. A, Sushrutha.S, Sudhir. P.M, Gangadhar. B. N, 2020).

Conclusion

This study aimed to understand if the different cultures in India have different perspectives and if different generations have different views of Ramayana. So, it is quite clear that most of the subjects of the study have very progressive thoughts and the results show that. Most of the subjects of the age group 15 – 30 and some of the people from the ages 30 – 60 have very feminist views and think some of the decisions made by Ram were for the greater good but he could have convinced his people to accept their queen and that the punishment she faced was quite horrifying and wrong. It was also seen that most south Indian cultures respect Ram but the north and western cultures have very varied responses.

The limitation of this study is that the sample is not big enough to show the contrast as well as, since the views are quite contradicting it is hard to pinpoint one particular view for one culture as the concepts of feminism are now not only accepted by the new generations but also by the older generation women and also since there is not much prior research on this topic the review of literature and information is quite incomplete.

The research concludes this study by saying that it is hard to detect one view for one culture or one generation since their answers are quite subjective. This is because every person goes through different experiences regardless of where they come from and if they were born in the same generation, but there are some similarities. Even if there isn't a way to pinpoint one view for either generation, we can see the lack of information in the new generation, for example, the concept of 'ram rajya' isn't seen or talked about by the newer generations. And since the new generations have learned from the older ones we can see the influence of that on the new generation's responses.

References

Alok. K, 2014, The participation- direction debate in leadership: Insights from Ramayana.

American Psychology Association, (N.D.), Culture.

Balamurali. E, Hariharasudan. A, 2021, Gender manifestation and implications of Sita in Ramayana.

Bhide. S, Kurhade. C et.al, 2020, Feasibility of using counselling techniques from Ramayana for managing negative emotions: an anecdotal review and analysis.

Goldman. R, (1980), Ramah Sahalaksmanah: psychological and literary aspects of the composite hero of Valmiki's Ramayana.

White. L, (N.D.), Culture.

CHAPTER FIVE

Sacred Bonds: Religion and Mental Health in Individualistic and Collectivistic Cultures

- **Megha M Nair**

Background

Religion is a set of organized beliefs, practices, and systems that most often relate to the belief and worship of a controlling force, such as a personal god or another supernatural being. Religion often involves cultural beliefs, worldviews, texts, prophecies, revelations, and morals that have spiritual meaning to members of the particular faith, and it can encompass a range of practices, including sermons, rituals, prayer, meditation, holy places, symbols, trances, and feasts. According to an estimate by the Pew Research Centre (2015), 84% of the world's population has some type of religious affiliation. Religion can serve a wide range of purposes. Religion can be a source of comfort and guidance. It can provide a basis for moral beliefs and behaviours. It can also provide a sense of community and connection to tradition. Some research even suggests that it may affect health. Prayer is the most essential and personal of religious experiences. It is central to religion as well as spirituality. Prayer is thoughts, attitudes and actions designed to express or experience connection to the sacred. Prayer is often a means to seek to identify the significance and/or meaning of life events, especially those of a negative nature, but those of a positive nature as well. Rituals offer structured practices that provide stability, order, and predictability, fostering feelings of security and comfort. Religious rituals foster community participation, promoting social support, belonging, and connectedness. they connect individuals to their cultural heritage and ancestral lineage, fostering a sense of continuity and belonging that enhances psychological well-being. The chapter also talks about the impact of religion on mental health and how it can be used to improve one's mental health. The impact of religion on mental health varies greatly throughout individuals as well as between diverse cultural and religious situations. It can provide moral direction, significance, and social support—all of which can have a beneficial psychological effect. It can, however, also bring challenges that must be properly negotiated and comprehended. Understanding the many ways that religion affects mental health is necessary to create supportive environments where people can benefit from their religious beliefs while addressing potential sources of pain or conflict.

Religion is a set of organized beliefs, practices, and systems that most often relate to the belief and worship of a controlling force, such as a personal god or another supernatural being. It frequently connects humanity to paranormal, transcendental, and spiritual elements. There are people who have religions and people who do not. We have the freedom to choose the religion we want to follow and how much to believe in it. India is a diverse country and has the greatest number of religions. Religious commitment is about how much an individual is devoted to their religion, how much time and belief is spent towards their particular belief. It is said that when one moves away from their roots such as living abroad away from your native, everything changes the lifestyle, routines and it is believed that your religious commitment also changes. This is different for different people. No matter where you are, one who truly is committed to something will not be disturbed just because there's a change. Most people have long valued their religious and spiritual beliefs, and these beliefs are typically linked to better health outcomes (Koenig & Larson, 2001). While spirituality is concerned with transcendent aspects of personal existence and refers to a personal, subjective aspect of religious experience, religion is conceptualized as a social entity that entails specific beliefs, customs, and boundaries (Hill & Pargament, 2008). Nonetheless, there is a shared emphasis on life's purpose and a motivating factor that encourages goal-oriented behavioural activation (Park, 2007). Contrarily, religiosity entails doing, feeling, and thinking in accordance with theological convictions that are upheld by a religious institution (Zinnbauer, et al., 1997). One of the best ways to gauge someone's level of religious fervour is to evaluate their level of intrinsic religiosity or religious desire. Those who have been regarded as having an inbuilt preference for religion are said to live out their beliefs and demonstrate how it has influenced every area of their lives (Joshi, & Kumari, 2011). The extent to which a person adheres to their religious principles, beliefs, and practices and applies them in daily life was defined as religious commitment by Worthington et al. in 2003. (p. 85). In other words, one's level of involvement in private religion, affiliation with a particular religion, engagement in religious activities, and the significance of their religious beliefs in their intrapersonal and interpersonal interactions are all examples of their level of religious commitment (Worthington et al., 2003). In order to examine more thoroughly how religion influences people—both favourably and negatively—and under what circumstances, Worthington (1988) employed a religious commitment model. He postulated that people who were most devoted to their religion would be the ones who were most positively affected by it (Worthington, 1988). Membership, involvement in religious activities, and allegiance to a religious faith are examples of factors that have been used to gauge religious devotion (Hill & Hood, 1999).

Inner serenity and self-realization are the main themes of intrapersonal religious practices. It is considered to be an intrinsic or internal manifestation of religiosity. While the inter-personal scale evaluates participation in formal religious activities. Even if people are religious, the type of religious commitment they have is not easily known. People who have interpersonal religious commitment are those who follow religion because they truly believe in it and follow it not because of societal force. Interpersonal religious commitment is those who are religiously committed because they are following their elders and societal norms and to fit in the group. Rustum Roy (1999), after giving a brief autobiographical background as an activist scientist and engineer provided a thorough analysis of the author's attempt to theoretically integrate science and religion. The key level to look for linkages in both science and religion is experience, not theory. Science as a theory is already in the process of reaching its own internal boundaries and due to the glaring shortcomings of reductionist science and technology, it is time for scientists and engineers to recommit to Einstein's vow to pursue research for the benefit of society. The growing acceptance of alternative medicine is a modern historical phenomenon that points to a developing, fundamental realignment of the relationship between science, technology, and society.

Collectivism and Religion

The intersection of religion and collectivism pertains to the integration of religious concepts and practices into communities that prioritize social peace, interdependence, and collective cohesiveness. In collectivist cultures, the interests of the individual are often subordinated to the benefit of the society. Religion in these contexts usually centers on rituals, beliefs, and collective worship. It is common to see adherence to religious traditions and practices as a way to maintain societal coherence and order. Cultural and social identities are closely associated with religious identity. Engaging in religion is more communal in nature, emphasizing social and familial responsibilities within the religious framework. Religion that is followed by the collectivistic cultures are Confucianism, Taoism, Buddhism and Hinduism. Confucianism places a strong emphasis on the role that leadership and education play in developing virtue. It is stressful to look out for those in the group. Through virtues, one can achieve enlightenment, or a good life. Taoism illustrates the concept of "The Way," which simultaneously relates to direction, movement, method, and cognition. Everyone is surrounded by Tao, which is an energy that must be experienced rather than merely taught. Buddhism makes reference to the teachings of the "Enlightened One," which maintain that all suffering in life stems from human attachment and desire. Still, the way the suffering ends might be through transcendence and ultimate awareness. It is vital to possess virtues like love, joy, compassion, and calmness. In Hinduism, the interdependence of all things is emphasized. It encourages everyone to live in harmony with one another and to look out for both their own and other people's best interests. Karma acts as a source of incentive for proper behaviour.

Collectivistic cultures have deeply ingrained customs, communal rituals, and a strong feeling of historical continuity that define their religious dedication. In these countries, religion plays a significant role that goes beyond individual belief systems to impact social structures, cultural conventions, and even political environments. In many collectivistic faiths, such as Confucianism, Buddhism, and Hinduism, religious dedication occurs through ritualistic participation and communal service. (Dumoulin Heinrich, 2005). They often highlight the interconnectedness of all life. For example, Hinduism's concept of Dharma describes duties and ethics, while Buddhism's Eightfold Path provides guidelines for moral behaviour, mental discipline, and knowledge. Family has a big impact on one's dedication to religion. Two fundamental Confucian practices that foster interpersonal peace and strong family bonds are ancestor worship and filial piety (Yao Xin Zhong, 2000). Religious commitment in collectivistic culture includes collective practices, there is a strong emphasis on communal rituals, festivals and temple visits. Religion plays a great role in the public life of individuals such as religious festivals are part of the national culture in countries like India and Japan (Casanova, 1994). The rituals connect individuals to their cultural heritage and ancestral lineage, fostering a sense of continuity and belonging that enhances psychological well-being. Religious teachings are frequently incorporated into education and daily life. Religious education is incorporated into the national curriculum in certain nations. (Miedema, Siebren, and Gerdien Bertram-Troost, 2015). Celebrations, regular rituals, and group worship are significant. Essential practices include yoga, meditation, and ancestral worship

Individualism and Religion

Individualism and religion refer to the interaction between religious beliefs and practices in communities that emphasize autonomy, self-expression, and individualism. Individualistic culture allows people to pursue their own goals and forge their own identities. In these contexts, religion usually revolves around the person's personal spiritual experiences, readings of religious texts, and relationship with God. People may become more individualized in their approach to faith as a result, seeking meaning and fulfilment in their own unique ways. The diversity and occasional nature of religious participation may be attributed to the large range of individual beliefs and behaviours. The three main religions followed by the individualistic culture are Christianity, Islam and Judaism. There has been a noticeable secularization tendency in collectivistic societies, as seen by a decline in religious affiliation and church attendance. Though it is also noticeable in North America, this tendency is more noticeable in Europe (Bruce,2002). Globalization and increased immigration have brought about a wider range of religious practices and beliefs. Increased interfaith dialogue and a wider acceptance of other religious traditions are results of this plurality.

Religious practice has shifted in Western culture toward individuality. It is more common for people to create their own spiritual paths than to rigorously follow established religions. (Roof, 1999). The number of individuals who describe themselves as not belonging to any religion—a term commonly used to refer to as "nones"—has significantly increased. This group is expanding, especially in North America and Europe (Voas, D., & Chaves, M. 2016). According to Pew research center (pew Research Center, 2015) In the United States 53% say religion is very important in their lives, Australia its 18%, United Kingdom is 10% and Russia is 16%. There is a separation between religion and state, they see religion as a private matter. Religious education happens in specific contexts like in church schools. Their public education is mostly secular. (Miedema, Siebren, and Gerdien Bertram-Troost, 2015). Make attending church, reading spiritual literature, and praying in private a priority. Life transitions and sacraments like marriage, baptism, and confirmation are important. Adam B. Cohen, Peter C. Hill (2007) proposed the theory that there are differences across religious civilizations in the individualistic and collectivistic aspects of religiousness and spirituality. Research 1 showed that whereas religion is mostly about personal beliefs for Protestants, it is more about community and biological descent for Jews. The notion that extrinsic religiosity stresses group and ritual while intrinsic religiosity is linked to personal religion is supported by the different relationships and endorsements of intrinsic and extrinsic religiosity shown by Jews, Catholics, and Protestants (Studies 2 and 3). For Jews and Protestants, respectively, significant life events were likely social, while for Catholics, they were religious (Study 4). In our conclusion, we provide three points of view to help you understand the complex relationships that exist between religion and culture.

Religion and Mental Health

Religion and mental health have a complex and nuanced relationship. Religious practices and beliefs can offer comfort and stability, but they can also raise anxiety and tension under certain circumstances. Disagreements among religious communities or problems with ambiguity or guilt can lead to psychological pain. Strict interpretations of religious ideas or pressure to live up to religious ideals can further exacerbate shame or feelings of inadequacy. Furthermore, religious beliefs about suffering, sin, and divine punishment can occasionally skew people's perceptions of mental illness, discouraging them from getting the appropriate medical or psychiatric care. It is well known that some components of religious practices and beliefs can either make mental health problems worse or better. Religious groups frequently offer social support systems that can act as a protective barrier against the damaging effects of hardship and stress, lowering the likelihood of mental illness (Koenig, 2012). For people dealing with mental health issues, religious beliefs and practices—such as prayer, meditation, and ritual—can work as coping mechanisms by offering comfort, hope, and a sense of purpose (Pargament, (2007). Participating in religious activities has been linked to enhanced resilience, which aids people in overcoming adversity and overcoming traumatic situations. (Koenig and Bonelli, 2013)

Gartner, J., Larson, D. B., & Allen, G. D. (1991). Findings from research on the connection between psychopathology and religious commitment have been contradictory. In a recent meta-analysis, Bergin (1983) discovered that 23%

of the research identified a negative association between religion and mental health, 47% found a favourable relationship, and 30% found no relationship at all. Our analysis of more than 200 papers led us to identify four additional tendencies. (a) The majority of studies examining the relationship between religious devotion and psychopathology have used so-called "soft variables'' in mental health research, such as paper-and-pencil personality assessments that aim to gauge theoretical constructs. Contrarily, the majority of research on religion and good mental health focuses on "hard variables, that is, "real life" behavioural events that are unmistakably significant and can be objectively observed and assessed. (b) Disorders involving the inability to control impulses are most frequently associated with low levels of religiosity, whereas disorders involving the inability to control impulses are most frequently associated with high levels of religiosity. (c) Behavioural rather than attitudinal indicators of religious participation are more strongly connected with mental health. (d) Some conflicting findings can be explained by distinctions between intrinsic and extrinsic religiosity.

Dale A. Matthews, MD; Michael E et. al. (1998) said that in the domains of prevention, coping, and recovery, the empirical literature from epidemiological and clinical investigations examining the link between religious influences and physical and mental health status was evaluated. These factors include frequency of religious attendance, private religious involvement, and relying on one's religious beliefs as a source of strength and coping. A minimum of 1 measure of the individuals' level of religious devotion and a minimum of 1 measure of their physical or mental health were utilized in empirical research from the published literature. Studies that looked at the role of religious devotion or religious involvement in sickness prevention, illness management, and illness recovery were highlighted in particular. A significant amount of empirical research that has been published indicates that religious devotion may be helpful in preventing mental and physical sickness, enhancing how people deal with mental and physical illness, and speeding up the healing process after illness. With better studies created specifically to look at the relationship between religious activity and health conditions, more still needs to be learned. Nonetheless, the information at hand indicates that clinicians who make a few minor adjustments to how patients' religious commitments are discussed in clinical practice may improve healthcare results.

Moreira-Almeida, Alexander et al. (2006) the research on the connection between religion and mental health was evaluated in this publication. The authors presented the key findings and recommendations of a more extensive systematic review that examined 850 papers on the connection between religion and mental health that were published in the 20th century and found using a variety of databases. Higher levels of religious involvement are positively correlated with psychological well-being indicators (life satisfaction, happiness, positive affect, and higher morale), as well as with lower rates of depression, suicidal thoughts and behaviors, and drug and alcohol abuse. The benefits of religious engagement on mental health are typically strongest for individuals who are under stress, such as the elderly, those with disabilities, and those who are unwell. Theoretical approaches to the relationship between religiosity and mental health are also covered, as well as the findings' implications for practice. There is proof that practicing a religion is typically linked to improved mental health. Our knowledge of the mediating variables in this relationship and how to apply it in clinical practice has to be strengthened.

Rose, T., Hope, M. O., et al. (2020) stated that many studies have been done on religion, and it is regularly used as a cultural and developmental resource. Yet, there has been little study on the relationship between non-organized religious activity (NRI) and psychological health in Black teens or Black children from other ethnic backgrounds. The subjects of this study, which examined this link, were 1 170 African American and Caribbean Black teenagers who participated in the National Survey of American Life-Adolescent Supplement survey. After correcting for study covariates, the major effects of NRI on life satisfaction, self-esteem, coping, and depressive symptoms were significantly seen, according to the results of moderated hierarchical regression (i.e., age, gender, family income, denomination, ethnicity, religious service attendance, and religious socialization). On any of the psychosocial well-being variables, there was no clear interaction effect between NRI and ethnicity. The results demonstrate that in this sample, NRI had a promoting effect. Even though no significant ethnicity and religiosity interaction effects were seen, the results indicate that NRI is a crucial intervention target to encourage improved psychosocial well-being among Black children in an effort to improve overall youth development.

Conclusion

Religion's impact on mental health is deeply intertwined with the cultural contexts of individualism and collectivism. In individualistic societies, where personal autonomy and self-expression are highly valued, religion can provide a sense of purpose and personal fulfilment, potentially enhancing mental well-being. Conversely, in collectivist cultures, where community and social harmony are emphasized, religious practices often foster strong social bonds and a sense of belonging, which can be protective against mental health issues. However, the pressures to conform to religious norms can also lead to stress and anxiety in both settings. Ultimately, the influence of religion on mental health is multifaceted, shaped by the interplay of cultural values, personal beliefs, and communal practices. Understanding this dynamic can help individuals and communities leverage the positive aspects of religion while mitigating potential negative effects on mental health.

References

APA PsycNet. (n.d.). https://psycnet.apa.org/record/2007-14177-000

Bruce, S. (2002). God is Dead: Secularization in the West. Wiley-Blackwell.

Casanova, José. Public Religions in the Modern World. University of Chicago Press, 1994

Cohen, A. B., & Hill, P. C. (2007). Religion as culture: religious individualism and collectivism among American Catholics, Jews, and Protestants. Journal of Personality, 75(4), 709–742. https://doi.org/10.1111/j.1467-6494.2007.00454.x

Dale A. Matthews, MD; Michael E. McCullough, PhD; David B. Larson, MD, MSPH; Harold G. Koenig, MD, MHSc; James P. Swyers, MA; Mary Greenwold Milano Arch Fam Med. (1998). Religious Commitment and Health Status , A Review of the Research and Implications for Family Medicine

Dumoulin, Heinrich. Zen Buddhism: A History, Volume 1: India and China. World Wisdom, 2005

Gartner, J., Larson, D. B., & Allen, G. D. (1991). Religious Commitment and Mental Health: A Review of Empirical Literature. Journal of Psychology and Theology, 19(1), 6–25.

Hill, P. C., & Pargament, K. I. (2008). Advances in the Conceptualization and Measurement of Religion and Spirituality: Implications for Physical and Mental Health Research. Psychology of Religion and Spirituality, S, 3-17.

Hill, P.C. and Hood Jr., R.W. (1999) Measures of Religiosity. Religious Education Press, Birmingham.

Jehad, Alaedein-Zawawi. (2015). Religious commitment and psychological well-being: Forgiveness as a mediator. European Scientific Journal February 2015 edition vol.11, No.5 ISSN: 1857 – 7881 (Print) e - ISSN 1857- 7431

Joshi, S., Kumari, S., & Jain, M. (2008). Religious belief and its relation to psychological well-being. ResearchGate. https://www.researchgate.net/publication/268277124

Koenig HG. Religion, spirituality, and health: the research and clinical implications. ISRN Psychiatry. 2012 Dec 16;2012:278730. doi: 10.5402/2012/278730. PMID: 23762764; PMCID: PMC3671693.

Masamichi Sasaki and Tatsuzo Suzuki . Changes in Religious Commitment in the United States, Holland, and Japan, Masamichi Sasaki and Tatsuzo Suzuki

Miedema, Siebren, and Gerdien Bertram-Troost. Religious Education and Social and Cultural Change: National and International Perspectives. Waxmann Verlag, 2015.

Moreira-Almeida, Alexander & Lotufo-Neto, Francisco & Koenig, Harold. (2006). Religiousness and Mental Health: A Review. Revista brasileira de psiquiatria (São

Paulo, Brazil : 1999). 28. 242-50. 10.1590/S1516-44462006000300018.

Roof, W. C. (1999). Spiritual Marketplace: Baby Boomers and the Remaking of American Religion. Princeton University Press.

Rose, T., Hope, M. O., Thurman, D., Forrester, P., & Rose, R. (2020). Non Organizational Religious Involvement and Psychosocial Well-Being Among African American and Caribbean Black Youth. Journal of Black Psychology, 46(5), 388–422.

Roy, R. (1999). Editorial. Bulletin of Science, Technology & Society, 19(5), 357–358. https://doi.org/10.1177/027046769901900501

Rustum Roy (1999) ,Religious commitment and its interaction with scientific professions: a low-church real-science, critique of "science" and "spirituality",Technology in Society,Volume 21,

Snyder, C. R., & Lopez, S. J. (2002). Positive psychology. Sage Publications

Stephen T. Mockabee, Joseph Quin Monson, J. Tobin Grant (2001).Measuring Religious Commitment Among Catholics and Protestants: A New Approach

Voas, D., & Chaves, M. (2016). Is the United States a Counterexample to the Secularization Thesis? American Journal of Sociology, 121(5), 1517-1556.

Wan Mohd Al Faizee Wan Ab Rahaman, Norazzila Shafie (2023) The Relationship Between Interpersonal and Intrapersonal Religious Commitment in Choosing Shariah Compliant Hospital in Malaysia Hamidah Mat*, Wan Mohd Al Faizee Wan Ab Rahaman, Norazzila Shafie

Yao, Xinzhong. An Introduction to Confucianism. Cambridge University Press, 2000

Zinnbauer, B. J., Pargament, K. I., Cole, B., Rye, M. S., Butter, E. M., Belavich, T. G., Hipp, K. M., Scott, A. B., & Kadar, J. L. (1997). Religion and Spirituality: Unfuzzying the fuzzy. In Society for the Scientific Study of Religion, Journal for the Scientific Study of Religion

CHAPTER SIX

Fulfilment of Faith: Nexus of Belief and Well-Being

- Sowmya D S

Background

Unwavering loyalty, belief, and trust are characteristics of mature faith, while life happiness is the degree to which an individual feels life rich, meaningful, full, or of excellent quality. One essential aspect of the human personality is religiosity. It significantly affects how people view the world, life, and themselves, as well as how they formulate ideas about what matters most in life. Numerous psychological and sociological theories help explain the connection between life contentment and religion maturity. According to social support theory, life satisfaction can be raised by the practical and emotional assistance that religious communities provide (Cohen & Wills, 1985). According to the theory of existential meaning, psychological health depends on having a strong sense of meaning and purpose in life, which is frequently obtained from religious beliefs (Frankl, 1984). The study's goal is to determine the relationship between life satisfaction and faith maturity.

Growing amounts of study have been conducted on life satisfaction since the 1980s, as it is a key component of subjective well-being (Diener, Oishi, & Lucas, 2015). Together with the increasing popularity of life satisfaction, subjective well-being, and various other related measures of quality of life, an increasing number of scales have been effectively developed to investigate the relationships between these attributes and other life events. Benson et al. (1993) separated faith into two categories: vertical and horizontal. A person's close relationship with God was described as vertical faith (Benson et al., 1993). This includes beliefs, a time of quiet prayer, fasting, studying the Bible, as well as other practices and ideas that are particularly focused on developing a close relationship with God. Benson et al. define horizontal faith as a person's care and concern for their environment. For example, horizontal faith includes a person's desire for justice in the globe as well as their efforts to feed the poor in their immediate community (Benson et al., 1993). Facebook use, genetics, income redistribution, and even cultural conceptions of happiness have all been linked to life satisfaction (Bastian, Kuppens, De Roover, & Diener, 2014).

Studies have discovered a positive correlation between religiosity dimensions like personal belief and practice (Leondari & Gialamas 2009) and a variety of indicators of subjective well-being, including life fulfillment, subjective physical and mental wellness, and experience of both positive and negative feelings. Furthermore, it has been found that religiosity is positively associated with a lower incidence of anxiety and depressive illnesses (Koenig et al.

1993).

Numerous subjects have been the subject of prior research, including the relationship between one's personal religious beliefs and psychological well-being. Greater amounts of intrinsic faith were associated with substantially lower scores for anxiety and depression, a lower likelihood of character pathology symptoms, and a stronger sense of ego strength than a smaller amount of intrinsic faith (Laurencelle, Abell, & Schwartz, 2002). There was notable variance within each of the connected categories, and these connections were only moderate. In a more recent study, Leonardi & Gialamis (2009) examined the relationship between religion & psychological well-being in a group of Greek Orthodox Christians. The study's findings showed a significant positive relationship between satisfaction with life and both church interest and attendance. However, they also found that those who prayed more frequently experienced higher levels of anxiety.

Psychological Context

In 1925, the first empirical investigations of subjective well-being began to emerge, despite the fact that philosophers and scientists had been discussing the purpose of life and happiness for thousands of years prior. The research of subjective well-being became more and more well-liked since then. However, since the 1980s, there has been an explosion of studies on subjective well-being due to the creation of reliable and valid scales for measuring subjective well-being and its components (Diener, Oishi, & Lucas, 2015). Diener et al (1985) attempted to construct a new life satisfaction measure that was more extensive than any that had been previously constructed (Diener et al., 1985).

This new scale takes into account the theory that factors other than personality or mental health—such as biological and environmental factors—may also contribute to life happiness. It evaluates not only sentiments and emotions but also overall satisfaction with life and the quality of life. Perceptions within a culture also have an impact on life satisfaction. Diener et al (1985) found that people who live in countries that prioritize happiness and positive tend to report greater levels of life satisfaction and subjective well-being. The study involved residents from 41 different countries. The satisfaction of the participants with many aspects of their life and society, both in general and in particular, was asked. Other academics have looked into the connections between optimism, life satisfaction, and self-esteem and a positive outlook. Positive orientation, also known as self-confidence or self-perception, is positively correlated with optimism, life satisfaction, and self-esteem (Alessandri, Caprara, & Tisak, 2012).

Religious Context

Numerous research have been conducted since 1985 to investigate the relationship among religion and subjective well-being, or the overall quality of life; however, no particular study has looked at the relationship between spiritual development and satisfaction with life. One such study is the one conducted by Leonardi and Gialamas (2009), which examines the connection between religion & subjective well-being. The primary research areas were the importance of religion and the frequency with which people attended church and engaged in prayer. Next, the connection between this and mental health, life satisfaction, and psychological well-being was looked at. They only saw shaky correlations between these, although this could be partially explained by the fact that people's actions did occasionally seem to match their beliefs. A mere 14% of participants reported attending church once more than a week, and 60% reported attending only sometimes, despite the fact that 78% of respondents stated that religion is essential or very important to them (Leonardi & Gialamis, 2009). Consequently, at least 64% of those surveyed stated that religion is extremely important or crucial to them.

This discrepancy raises the question of whether the results would change if participants' opinions about the importance of religion and their actions aligned. Healthy spiritual lives are linked to decreased incidences of depression, according to study (Hawkins, Tan, & Turk, 1999). In a separate study, participants ranging in age from 18 to 86 demonstrated a favourable correlation between their belief in a loving God and their emotional well-being. Furthermore, research has demonstrated a clear connection between substance abuse and belief in a kind, loving God (Brelsford et al., 2009). This shows that traits of overall satisfaction with life and variables influencing overall health encompass both emotional well-being and addictive tendencies. A favourable relationship between one's personal religious beliefs and psychological well-being was discovered by another study (Laurencelle, et al., 2002). Focusing on the strength of the ego, superego courage, anxiety, depression, as well as character pathology, the researchers found that participants with mild to high levels in religious faith outperformed those with low levels of religious faith significantly in each of these categories. According to Laurencelle et al. (2002), these results point to a relationship between psychological well-being and religious belief. Other research indicates a positive correlation between psychological well-being and religion (Hawkins, Tan, & Turk, 1999). There is a wealth of data linking psychology and faith, but not much research has particularly examined the connection between life satisfaction and faith development.

Adolescents' Faith Maturity and Life Satisfaction: Faith maturity is the absorption of religious teachings and how they affect an individual's conduct and decision-making. It goes beyond a person's connection with a religion or their attendance at religious services. A theoretical foundation for comprehending how faith changes from infancy to adulthood is provided by Fowler's Stages of Faith Development, which postulate that faith maturity during adolescence might affect life satisfaction as a whole (Fowler, 1981). Higher degrees of faith maturity in teenagers have been linked to favourable psychological outcomes, including less anxiety and despair, increased self-esteem, and improved coping mechanisms (King & Furrow, 2004). These favourable results are linked to the moral guidance, feeling of purpose, and encouraging community that are frequently seen in religious settings. One important measure of adolescents' general wellbeing and mental health is their level of life satisfaction. It represents a person's emotional and cognitive assessment of their life as a whole. Adolescents' life happiness is influenced by a variety of factors, such as extracurricular activities, academic achievement, peer interactions, and family dynamics (Huebner, 2004). Prior research has demonstrated a favourable relationship between life satisfaction and religious participation. According to Holder et al. (2000), for example, teenagers who engage in religious activities typically report higher levels of satisfaction and fulfilment. Religious communities offer social support and a sense of belonging that might improve life happiness by encouraging resilience and an optimistic view on life.

Conclusion

The correlation between life satisfaction and religion maturity has been studied, and the results demonstrate the important role that religiosity plays in young people's psychological and emotional development. Adolescents with both vertical and horizontal aspects of faith maturity get moral instruction, a strong sense of purpose, and support from their community. Positive psychological results, such decreased anxiety and sadness, increased self-esteem, and improved coping mechanisms, are greatly enhanced by these factors. According to the research, teenagers who are more mature in their beliefs typically lead happier lives. This is explained by the encouraging atmosphere that religious societies create, the feeling of community that they foster, and the organized belief systems that give life direction and meaning. This study adds to the expanding body of research on the relationship between religiosity and wellbeing, providing insightful information for future studies and treatments targeted at promoting the development of adolescents.

References

Alessandri, G., Caprara, G. V., & Tisak, J. (2012). The unique contribution of positive orientation to optimal functioning. European Psychologist.

Bastian, B., Kuppens, P., De Roover, K., & Diener, E. (2014). Is valuing positive emotion associated with life satisfaction? Emotion, 14(4), 639.

Benson, P. L., Donahue, M. J., & Erickson, J. A. (1993). The faith maturity scale: Conceptualization, measurement, and empirical validation. Research in the social scientific study of religion, 5(1), 1-26.

Brelsford, G. M., Marinelli, S., Ciarrochi, J. W., & Dy-Liacco, G. S. (2009). Generativity and spiritual disclosure in close relationships. Psychology of Religion and Spirituality, 1(3), 150.

Cohen, S., & Wills, T. A. (1985). Stress, social support, and the buffering hypothesis. Psychological bulletin, 98(2), 310.

Diener, E. D., Emmons, R. A., Larsen, R. J., & Griffin, S. (1985). The satisfaction with life scale.

Diener, E., Oishi, S., & Lucas, R. E. (2015). National accounts of subjective well-being. American psychologist, 70(3), 234.

Ebstyne King, P., & Furrow, J. L. (2008, August). Religion as a resource for positive youth development: religion, social capital, and moral outcomes. In Meeting of the Society for Research in Child Development, Apr, 2001, Minneapolis, MN, US; A previous version of this article was presented at the aforementioned conference. (No. 1, p. 34). Educational Publishing Foundation.

Fowler, J. W. (1981). Stages of faith: The psychology of human development and the quest for meaning. Harper & Row.

Frankl, V. E. (1985). Man's search for meaning. Simon and Schuster.

Hawkins, R. S., Tan, S. Y., & Turk, A. A. (1999). Secular versus Christian inpatient cognitive-behavioral therapy programs: Impact on depression and spiritual well-being. Journal of psychology and theology, 27(4), 309-318.

Holder, M. D., Coleman, B., & Wallace, J. M. (2010). Spirituality, religiousness, and happiness in children aged 8–12 years. Journal of happiness studies, 11, 131-150.

Huebner, E. S. (2004). Research on assessment of life satisfaction of children and adolescents. Social indicators research, 66, 3-33.

Journal of personality assessment, 49(1), 71-75.

Koenig, H. G., George, L. K., & Peterson, B. L. (1998). Religiosity and remission of depression in medically ill older patients. American Journal of Psychiatry, 155(4), 536-542.

Laurencelle, R. M., Abell, S. C., & Schwartz, D. J. (2002). The relation between intrinsic religious faith and psychological well-being. The International Journal for the Psychology of Religion, 12(2), 109-123.

Leondari, A., & Gialamas, V. (2009). Religiosity and psychological well-being. International journal of psychology, 44(4), 241-248.

Across the Veil: Diverse Rituals and Practices in Death Ceremonies

- Snehalata Patil

Background

There are numerous ways for someone to pass away. One of those inescapable and ambiguous concepts, death and dying can be interpreted in so many different ways by different people, but ultimately, they all mean the same thing. Precisely how one passes away varies. There are several facets to death. The shutting down of vital organs is one definition of biological death. An individual's body stops functioning each organ as they go through the process of dying. Due to the damage to their digestive system, they may cease eating normally and their breathing may become more irregular and noisier. When people cease visiting a chronically ill person who is about to pass away, social death happens. Because everyone is aware that there is no cure for a terminal illness, sometimes even medical professionals stop spending a lot of time with the patient. Because people feel uneasy around those who are going to die, many of these social deaths take place. Can you help those who are dying in any way? When a person begins to accept their mortality and begins to psychologically retreat from their surroundings, they experience psychological death. They can begin to show very little interest in current events and other things going on around them. This may occur well in advance of biological death. There are five primary psychological stages when attempting to accept someone's terminal illness. It also applies to people whose loved ones are suffering from a terminal illness. Denial, rage, bargaining, sadness, and acceptance are some of these psychological stages (Kubler-Ross, 1960). We are all aware that there is no one correct method to grieve or accept the way things are. One can go through these phases more than once and not always in the specified order.

A Study in Exploration of Cultural Differences in Death Ceromonies

This study aims to understand the differences in the procedure of burial or funeral and the stages of grief in different cultures. 20 people, 10 of the age group 17 to 25 and the other 10 of the age group 26 to 60 were asked a set of questions regarding their unique way of dealing with a death in their family and practicing its rituals. Questions included the rituals and superstitious beliefs in their family or community regarding death and the practices. We know everyone deals with death in their way. Few go through the stages of grief while few communities just happen to move on after someone's death. This study aims to understand how people from different cultures have their way of practicing their rituals and ways of sending the deceased off.

According to archaeological studies, Hindus of the Vedic era screamed out, "Away, go away, O death! Injure not our sons, not our men". The Nayars of Malabar held that removing the dead's bones and ashes brought them spiritual peace and released the living from their wounds. Hindu traditions dictate that the male member of the family—son, brother, or father— always ignites the funeral pyre. Whereas other religions, including Christianity, practice burial, Hindus invariably burn the body. In the culture of Khasis, when an individual dies at a distance from home and whose body hasn't burned although it's supposed to be according to the rituals, the clan member or the children of the deceased is supposed to take three to four seeds or cowries to a place where three roads meet and then throw the seeds into the air and yell a pray that goes "to alle noh ba ngin sa lum sa kynshew noh ia phi" which means "come, now we will collect you". Here the seeds represent the bones of the departed.

In Tibet, people practice something called "sky burial". This is because they believe that dead bodies are nothing but discarded shells and they should be fed to animals as a form of charity. Cremation is also followed but there's very little wood in Tibet which is why people follow sky burial more. It involves chopping up a dead body and placing it at a peak which can help vultures and other omnivore animals to feed on it. In Madagascar, people practice a tradition called Famadihaha, which translates to "dancing with the dead" and referred to as "turning of the bones". This tradition involves opening the tombs of the deceased once every five to seven years to rewrap them with fresh burial clothes and spray perfume. It includes relatives getting together for drinks, dancing with the bodies just before the sun sets. Then the body is put back into the tomb for the next five to seven years. The belief behind this tradition is that humans cannot move on to the next life until their body is completely decomposed. Exhuming the body and repeating this process every five to seven years can accelerate the process of decomposition of the body.

In New Orleans, a tradition called Jazz Funerals is followed. While Americans have a somber funeral, this one perfectly blends the grief and joy. It involves marching from the funeral home to the cemetery. In the start they play slow sorrowful songs but once the body is buried, everything shifts to an upbeat vibe. In the Philippines, there are various ways people proceed with the rituals for the deceased and that depends on the region and the ethnic group they belong to. The Benguet people living in the Northern Philippines typically blindfold the deceased and keep them next to the home's main entrance. The Tinguian people dress the deceased in their best clothes, make them sit on a chair, light a cigarette and keep it between their lips and keep them like this for several weeks.

In Sadaga, coffins are kept at places that are hard to reach or on mounted places because they believe that if the coffin is closer to the sky, it is easier for the dead to attain heaven. Before placing the body in the coffin, it is placed on a chair with the help of vines and leaves covered with a blanket. In the meantime, people come to pay respect to the deceased and the family. Just before the body is hoisted on a high-altitude place, the mourners let the fluids from the deceased body fall over them because they believe that it is good luck. In Ghana, a popular tradition called "Fantasy Coffin's" is practiced. Here the dead can get various kinds of coffins, differing by shape and size. It is carved in a way that depicts what job the deceased did or what they loved the most. In this culture, it is believed that the dead are more powerful than the living, so families try to do everything they can to ensure that their departed ones are happy with them. They often spend a lot of money on coffins due to the customization (Goldade, 2017).

According to the "2011 Census of India", Hinduism is the most prevalent religion in India, with 79.8% of the population practicing it, and 14.2% practice Islam. With more than 1.5 billion adherents, Islam is the second most popular religion in the world, and the top three nations where Muslims are concentrated are India, Indonesia, and Pakistan. Hinduism is the third most popular religion in the world, with approximately 1 billion adherents, most of whom are concentrated in India, Sri Lanka, Nepal, and other nations. Although both of these religions are followed in India, they have separate funeral customs and beliefs, however there are some commonalities between them and their respective civilizations. In Hindu traditions, if a person appears to be on their deathbed, they and their loved ones will typically recite a "mantra" that they believe will console them. In Islam, family members assist the dying individual in reciting the Shahada, a phrase that essentially states, "There is no God but Allah, and Muhammad is prophet of Allah." Muslims believe that the body should be buried within 24 hours of passing. Hinduism permits visitors to view the deceased in an open or translucent coffin for the final time, but touching them is not permitted. White casual clothing is preferred because it is considered bad luck to wear black to a Hindu funeral. When priests and close family members gather for the rites, they all pray, sing hymns, and chant mantras. Instead of a funeral, Hindus typically have a cremation ceremony. The corpse is placed on a piece of wood, and the Karta, who is often the eldest male in the home, goes three times around it anticlockwise while dousing it with holy water. This occurred in the past when cremation was performed manually instead of today's crematoriums. But just as before, people continue to sprinkle holy water on the body. The Karta may now press the crematorium's start button. Although cremation is forbidden in Islamic societies.

They adhere to the custom of interment and funeral rites for the deceased. At the mosque facing Mecca, prayers are said for the deceased. Everyone heads to the burial plot after the prayers are over to complete the necessary burial preparations. In both the religions and their distinct traditions, only men are traditionally permitted to attend the funeral service, the cremation, or the burial. In Hindu societies, the period of grieving typically lasts until the thirteenth day following the death. Crows are the favorite food of the departed in many cultures, thus people feed them for 13 days under the assumption that the corpse is doing so. In Islam, the period of mourning typically lasts for 40 days, however a widow may grieve for up to a year. She is forbidden from conversing with potential suitors for her next marriage. While sobbing out of grief is permissible, rejecting Allah is not. This is in contrast to breaking things.

Findings

This study aimed to determine whether there were significant cultural or intercultural disparities in the performance of rituals following the death of a family member. For this study, a qualitative research design was chosen. Twenty persons were involved in the qualitative data analysis, who were divided into two age groups (17 to 25 and 26 to 60). Throughout the session, these topics were brought up frequently by both age groups. The semi-structured interview's findings are listed under the relevant themes and results. The findings must only be indicative of the interviewees, it is crucial. However, it gave detailed descriptions of their ideas and attitudes in addition to their opinions. By responding to the series of open-ended questions and actively taking part in the interview, each participant contributed information. Five main themes/outcomes were formed namely, Aid and Assistance, Rituals, Social aspects, Symbolism, and Bureaucracy.

One of the main things a person who is severely ill and is on their deathbed would need is proper aid and assistance until their last breath. Being beside someone who is going to die is not easy but there are few things a person can do to help them as best as they can. There are deathbed etiquettes usually followed when one doesn't know how to handle a situation so heart-wrenching. A few things like listening to what the person wants because you are probably the only support, they have, if something seems different or concerning, one must seek help by informing the doctors or the authority. Make sure that their last wish can come true, usually, they wish for the whole family to get together and other minimalist ideas. Make them feel comfortable and reassure them that they can let go if it is a lot of pain to bear. Few people believed that praying and offering to God could help them provide care and safety for their ill relative.

In this study, the participants were asked questions like What did people in your family do when someone was seriously ill? and Who would normally look after the dying relative? and Where and how would the person want to spend the last moments of their life? One participant, when asked a question, said they instead went to the mosque and started praying regularly and very often and most of the prayers were like "if she recovers we'll read the Quran, give food to the orphans and all".

The majority of India's population consists of Hindus who prefer cremating the body after someone's death. But the Muslim population, which is about 15%, prefers to bury the body. They strongly do not believe in burning the body. Generally, tradition holds that the body needs to be cremated or buried within the first 24 hours in Hindu, Islam, Jain and within 3 days in Sikh. In this study, when asked about ritual proceedings in their culture, one participant answered Soon after death, we'll keep the body in such a way that it is facing towards the west side. It is because our Mecca, the pilgrimage, is in that direction. Then we keep some weight on the stomach of the deceased so that the waste inside has to come out. And finally, we will clean all those unwanted things and we'll take the body for the bath. For a lady's death, the ladies of the house do the rituals while in a man's death, the men of the house do the rituals. The main four areas they clean are front, back, face and armpits. Then for both male and female bodies, they cover it with a green piece of cloth. Then they wrap it and just keep the face exposed.

The participant also says, the thing is, it is a saying that if you are born you have to be born in a Brahmin family so that you'll be respected when you're alive but when you die you're supposed to die in an Islam family because you'll get more respect after your death. It's because of how precisely, honestly we take care of the body after their death.

When a Hindu participant was asked about their rituals and proceedings they mentioned they believe that in our family, their ancestors come in the form of crows so they usually keep food outside after the ceremony and on the 13th day as well they serve the whole family. They call the whole family for the ceremony and feed all of them. Quite a few cultures within the Hindus believe in this particular ritual.

Another participant gave a brief explanation, we do something called "mundan" where the son of the family gets bald and is made to sit isolated and not allowed to eat salt or sugar content for 3 to 5 days. The person is also not allowed to have any contact with others so he's made to sit behind a wall of bamboo trees.

Primary family plays a very important role in anyone's life. At one's birth and death, if your family is around you, you are considered to be lucky. It is said that if you have your family and close ones by your side when you are on your deathbed, you've truly lived life. Few believed that prayers and offerings could be used as a form of aid to the ill. Few think if their close ones are around during their last hours, and they assist them, that is their aid. In a few cultures, relatives do the arrangement of the funeral and other rituals instead of the primary family because it is believed that it will be too hard on them. In this study, the participants were asked questions like What did people in your family do when someone was seriously ill? and Who would normally look after the dying relative? and Where and how would the person want to spend the last moments of their life? A lot of the participants responded saying that friends, family and close relatives are important and some as well said that once you see every loved one of yours for the last time, you won't have any regrets after dying.

There are a few symbols that have significance to the family or the dead in different cultures. When the participants were asked about their beliefs on 'Pitru Paksha', a lunar day where Hindus offer food to their ancestors that they believe come in the form of crows. It is also known as 'Shradh'. As depicted in the Garuda Purana,

Shradh holds a major significance because it is believed that the soul of the deceased is traveling to Yamapuri on the 14th day and reaches there in 17 days. Then travel for 11 months to reach Yamraja's court. But, the soul doesn't get any food or edibles and hence we perform Pitru Paksha so the souls can satisfy their hunger and thirst. The Shradh Pooja is addressed by the men, including a priest. The pooja includes feeding the poor and the needy. The food prepared for them is also given to crows, dogs and cows.

1. Crows - In Hindus, it is believed that the dead or deceased come to meet their family in the form of crows. It is also considered that crows are messengers of 'Pitra Loka' (translated - the land of the deceased).
2. Ants - In Hindus, ants are also fed in a shradh pooja. Ants are considered as elements of fire so feeding sweet to them can bring blessings to our ancestors.
3. Dogs - In Hindus, it is believed that dogs guard the doors of hell and heaven. A dog is considered as an element of water.
4. Cows - In Hindus, cows already have a very high status due to religious affiliations. So, feeding cows after someone's death is really considered auspicious.

The 13th day is a very important day to all the Hindus. It's called 'Terhavin' in North India which means 13th. These days are considered to be given for the family of the deceased to mourn. During these 13 days, the family of the deceased is considered to be impure and have to be bound by certain rules and behaviors. When the participants were asked for the significance of the 13th day, they said I'm not very sure about the significance but we distribute food to the whole village and amongst the poor and to the loved ones of the deceased.

Another person who belonged to one of the Hindu cultures, said We serve food to five women of the family and one child on the 13th day. They are made to sit in front of the photo frame of the deceased, the food is also served for the photograph. Then, once the women are done eating, one of the members of the primary family of the deceased has to eat from the plate kept in front of the photo.

A lot of participants talked about how the first thing their family did when someone died was to issue a death certificate. One participant mentioned that my uncle was admitted in a completely different state because he had some rare disease and only that particular place could give him the right treatment. The participant mentioned that they got the certificate after a few days and they couldn't go further with the rituals and proceedings without a death certificate.

Another participant talked about their grandfather's death and said We had to wait for the death certificate to be issued. It was during the covid time and hence they delayed issuing the death certificate for a few days. We couldn't start the rituals or do the further proceedings without the death certificate.

A death certificate usually helps people close their bank account. A death certificate usually also lets people know the cause of death and final disposition. In India, it is necessary to have a death certificate according to the law. Only after your name is registered in the list, can you proceed with the rituals and funeral for that person. It generally takes 4 to 5 working days to get a death certificate issued.

Conclusion

During the study, few participants showed signs of ethnocentrism because they started to compare their religion/culture to others and mentioned how better their religion/culture was in those aspects. This study was conducted on people with different cultural background. Due to the fact that India's population among Hindu's higher than that of other religions, finding other cultures and religions wasn't easy and they cannot be representative of the larger population. Since the age group was 17 to 25, many of the people did not know much about their cultural background or rituals and traditions of their culture. During the session, a lot of the participants understood the insights of their culture and the traditions they follow. The study helped in summarizing the rituals and traditions different cultures practice when their loved one is dead. This study also helped the interviewer and the participants understand how important one's life is and how carefully their family will take care of them once they are gone. The study was more on an emotional basis than practical. Few of the participants teared up during the session by remembering their loved one, who they witnessed pass away. This paper can serve as a guide for all the youngsters and children who do not know much about their culture and their traditions followed when there is a death in their family.

References

Adetunji, J. (2021). Indias are forced to change their rituals for their dead as COVID-19 rages through cities and villages. Cremation grounds and colonial rule.

Bendann, E. (2017). Death Customs: An Analytical Study of Burial Rites. Chapter III Disposal of the Dead (45-48).

Binford, L. R. (2018). Mortuary Practices: Their study and their potential. Memoirs of the society for American Archaeology.

Gohri, R. (2022). Death Certificate for Property Claim and How to Obtain Death Certificate. Magicbricks, Death Certificates.

Goldade, J. (2017). Cultural Spotlight : Indian Funeral Traditions. Religious beliefs, Visitations and Funeral services.

Manjari AS, Veena N (2016), "To Talk or Not To Talk": Parents Perspectives on Sex Education, International Journal of Indian Psychology, Volume 4, Issue 1, No. 80

N.D. (n.a.). The Art Of Dying Well. Deathbed étiquettes.

N.D. (2020). Funeral Rites across Different Cultures. The symbols of Death, The significance of color, The symbolism of hair.

N.D. (2020). How Burial Traditions and Funerals Differ by Culture. La Vista Memorial Park and Mortuary.

Saxena, N. (2020). All About Pitru Paksha (Shradh) : History, significance, facts and destinations.

Shaffer, G. D. (2005). NANTICOKE INDIAN BURIAL PRACTICES: CHALLENGES FOR ARCHAEOLOGICAL INTERPRETATION. Archaeology of Eastern North America, 33, 141–162.

CHAPTER EIGHT

Cycles of Tradition: Cultural Perspectives on Menstruation in India

- Deepika M

Background

Menstruation is a topic that is vastly researched upon in a physiological sense, however there is very limited information and research on the cultural implications and understanding of this phenomenon. It is important to cater to the cultural aspects of menstruation as well as its physiological effects to develop a more inclusive and elaborate understanding of how stigma can be tackled. The prevalence of stigma can be attributed vastly to the lack of knowledge, accessibility to information, exposure and improper education on menstruation that focuses on explaining the phenomena in a manner such that it is understood by the larger population. Understanding how women from different cultures view menstruation aids in identifying methods that can be incorporated by outreach programs and awareness campaigns to structure their agenda in a manner such that it is more relatable, acceptable and beneficial to the community they are targeting. The results of this study can also be further interpreted to provide a more inclusive education on the topic and to build infrastructure that normalises menstruation whilst being a vital factor in establishing sanitary standards at multiple locations increasing the accessibility for women when in need. A study such as this provides further insights to analyse the efficiency of various government run efforts to provide resources and infrastructure to the larger population, and also incorporates education and outreach schemes to target lower socioeconomic status locations that do not have access to educational resources that aid in alleviating the stigma around menstruation.

The knowledge and interpretations that people and communities give to diverse cultural practices, beliefs, and artefacts are referred to as cultural interpretation. It entails examining the ways in which diverse cultural groups view, regard, and interpret their reality, including language, symbols, rituals, practices, and norms. The historical, social, political, and economic settings, as well as individual and group experiences, beliefs, and values, all have an impact on how cultures are interpreted. Understanding cultural interpretations is crucial for valuing and respecting variety, advancing intercultural dialogue, and creating successful plans for resolving cultural disputes. Menstruation is a typical aspect of the hormone-controlled menstrual cycle, which affects women of reproductive age once a month on average. Bleeding, which can vary in strength and colour, is a characteristic of menstruation, which typically lasts for 3 to 7 days. It is essential for fertility and childbearing, and it is an indication that the female reproductive system is operating appropriately.

The cultural interpretation of menstruation in India is shaped by various factors such as social, religious, and cultural understandings. Menstrual habits and beliefs are significantly influenced by Hinduism, which is the country's main religion. According to the traditional Hindu viewpoint, menstruation is a sign of impurity, and women should abstain from participating in religious activities while they are menstruating. Several cultural traditions and beliefs that link menstruation to filth and pollution support this viewpoint. Menstruation has always been surrounded by myths and taboos that keep women from participating in many facets of sociocultural life. The subject has always been taboo in India. Menstruation-related taboos, which are prevalent in many cultures, have an influence on girls and women's emotional well-being, attitude, way of life, and, most significantly, health. The difficulty of confronting the menstrual taboos and cultural stereotypes is made even more difficult by the lack of knowledge and awareness about puberty, menstruation, and reproductive health among females.

Rituals during Menstruation

Menstruation is surrounded by cultural taboos and customs that are unique to many ethnicities and faiths. Different cultures and religions follow different practices during menstruation that have been passed on from generations to generations. The majority of current methods may not make much sense right now, yet they previously had a purpose.

Bengali women who are menstruating are encouraged to relax and refrain from strenuous physical activity. They are also forbidden from touching pickle jars and from taking part in religious rituals or festivities. To mark the end of their periods, women apply vermillion on each other's foreheads as part of a ritual purifying procedure called "Sindoor Khela" after the menstrual cycle has finished. During a woman's menstrual cycle, Tamil women are not permitted to use any kitchen appliances, prepare food, or handle any culinary utensils. Moreover, women are not permitted inside the shrine while they are menstruating.

Women in Manipuri culture are expected to spend three days alone during their menstrual cycle. They must adhere to a rigorous diet and are forbidden from touching anybody, even members of their own family. Menstruating women in Naga society are expected to stay in a separate "maram," or chamber or home, outside the community. Also, they are forbidden from touching or cooking for anybody, even family members. Menstruating women are not permitted to handle pickles or spices, cook, or take part in any religious activity in Marwari tradition. When the menstrual period is over, they must also take a bath before using the kitchen or engaging in any other activity.

Many young women and girls have limitations in their everyday lives just because they are having their period. For urban females, the main limitation during menstruation is to avoid the "puja" chamber, but for rural girls, it is to avoid the kitchen. Girls and women who are menstruating are likewise forbidden from praying or touching sacred objects. This myth's fundamental premise is also rooted in societal notions of the impure nature of menstruation. Menstruation-related cultural norms and religious taboos are frequently made worse by historical connotations with bad spirits, humiliation, and embarrassment related to sexual reproduction. In some cultures, women bury the clothing they wear for their periods to keep bad spirits from using them.

Menstrual Hygiene Management

The diverse customs and viewpoints of menstrual hygiene in various Indian cultures and locations focus on concerns including the availability of clean water, sanitary facilities, and reasonably priced menstruation products, as well as the difficulties and potential for improving menstrual health and cleanliness. Access to period products and knowledge of menstruation vary greatly around the globe. Tampons, pads, menstrual cups, and pantiliners are among the feminine hygiene supplies that are often widely accessible in developed nations. Access to menstruation products, especially disposable ones, is extremely restricted in other regions, notably in portions of Africa, India, and Southeast Asia. The majority of women in these regions use reusable cloths to absorb menstrual blood, but they frequently lack access to facilities or the right cleaning supplies to effectively clean dirty cloths. Even in nations where goods are readily accessible, certain women may still struggle to get access to them, especially those who are homeless or live in poverty.

The cost of menstruation products is one of the main obstacles in India. Commercial sanitary products like tampons and pads can be somewhat costly, especially for those who are poor, and many women simply cannot afford to buy them. Menstrual products are also not readily available in some portions of the nation, notably in rural areas where access to healthcare and other resources is constrained. Women's health and wellbeing can be significantly impacted by a lack of access to menstruation products. Women who are unable to adequately manage their periods may face shame, humiliation, and embarrassment in addition to an increased risk of infection and other health issues. Their mental health and general quality of life may suffer as a result, which can create a feeling of exclusion and loneliness.

Menstruating women may be expected to stay away from other community members during their periods in some societies because they are seen as filthy or unclean. These attitudes can make it more difficult for women to get the knowledge and tools they require to adequately manage their periods and can also contribute to a lack of awareness and education about basic menstrual hygiene practices. It is crucial to provide more knowledge and instruction about menstrual hygiene in order to solve this problem, especially in regions where cultural beliefs may function as a roadblock to appropriate menstrual hygiene practices. This may entail collaborating with local leaders and educators to raise awareness of the value of menstruation hygiene and to dismantle cultural taboos and assumptions that may contribute to a lack of knowledge and education.

Cultural Beliefs and Practices

The significance of menarche, or the start of menstruation, differs between groups and geographical areas in India. Yet, it is seen as a significant rite of passage for girls in many cultures, signifying their entry into womanhood. Girls may be lauded and congratulated for attaining this milestone since menarche is frequently viewed as a symbol of fertility and possible parenthood. The event of "menarche" is ritualised in many cultures and celebrated as a grand occasion with friends, relatives and close members of the extended family. These rituals might involve eating, gift-giving, and the girl being decked up in costume and jewels. In other situations, the girl could be segregated for a while while being instructed about menstruation hygiene and other facets of femininity by more experienced women in the neighbourhood. In addition, there could be variations in how menarche is seen according to elements including socioeconomic status, religion, and location.

Menstruating women may be subject to a number of restrictions and taboos in some cultures in India because menstruation is seen to be a sign of impurity and purity. These behaviours and beliefs can have a substantial influence on women's lives since they are frequently firmly rooted in cultural and religious traditions. Menstruating women may be restricted from accessing specific parts of the home or taking part in certain activities in some societies because they are perceived as being filthy or unclean. During their period, they might also have to follow particular customs or refrain from certain foods or activities. These limitations may result in social exclusion and stigma, as well as prevent access to possibilities for career and education.

Stigma and Discrimination

The exclusion of menstruation women from religious events and settings is a frequent instance of prejudice. Several temples and other religious buildings forbid women from entering while they are menstruating because they believe they are unclean. The impression that menstruation is something disgusting or filthy may be reinforced by this exclusion, which may have detrimental effects on women's self-worth. The inability women obtain facilities and goods for menstruation hygiene is another instance of prejudice. Women often struggle to maintain their menstrual hygiene because they lack access to sanitary, private restrooms in many areas of India. Health problems and social marginalisation may result from a shortage of inexpensive, safe menstruation products. Menstruation is frequently stigmatised and tabooed, which can result in a lack of knowledge and instruction on menstrual hygiene and health. Because of the shame and prejudice connected with menstruation, this ignorance can encourage harmful actions and attitudes.

Menstrual Health and Well-being

Despite the widespread use of menstrual hygiene practices, many regions of the country still lack awareness of and education about menstruation health and cleanliness. This emphasises the necessity of paying more attention to menstrual hygiene and health, especially in the context of culturally sensitive techniques that take into consideration the various practices and beliefs of other cultures. Just 42% of teenage women in rural India solely adopted sanitary procedures, with significant regional differences at the state and district levels. At the state level, 85% of Tamil Nadu and 23% of Uttar Pradesh used only sanitary procedures. At the district level, there was much more variance seen. In rural India, there was a pronounced north-south split in the adoption of only sanitary procedures. When individual and community-level characteristics were taken into account, the findings of multilevel logistic regression showed that there was a significant amount of heterogeneity in the exclusive use of sanitary procedures at the community level.

Around one-fifth of all teenage women live in India. Sadly, the majority of them, particularly those who reside in rural regions, frequently encounter several limitations that impede their agency and autonomy. Teenage girls in India drop out of school in the millions each year as a result of physical limitations, a shortage of toilets and disposal facilities, and feelings of embarrassment brought on by the smell and stains of menstrual blood. Poor menstrual hygiene habits are made worse by the widespread misinformation around puberty and menstruation, the lack of availability to menstrual hygiene products, and the inadequate access to water, sanitation, and hygiene facilities.

The Ministry of Health and Family Welfare has launched a programme known as menstrual hygiene scheme, to encourage teenage females in rural regions between the ages of 10 and 19 to practise good menstrual hygiene. The programme was first put into effect in 2011 in 107 chosen districts across 17 States, where rural teenage girls were given a pack of six sanitary towels named "Free Days" at a cost of Rs. 6. From 2014, funding under the National Health Mission has been given to States and UTs for the decentralised purchase of sanitary napkin packs for distribution to rural teenage girls at a discounted rate of Rs 6 for a pack of 6 napkins.

There is a problem that requires more focus and funding, expanding access to menstruation products in both developed and developing nations. A collaborative effort between policymakers in each nation, the business community, and advocates for women's rights will be necessary to improve the menstrual experience for women throughout the world.

Conclusion

Cultural practices and beliefs have a big impact on how women there view and experience menstruation. In India, various communities and areas have very distinct cultural views and customs about menstruation, which reflects the broad variety of cultural traditions that exist there. Despite the fact that menstruation taboos and limitations are common in India, a significant push to disprove these notions and advance menstrual hygiene and health has emerged in recent years. To increase knowledge of menstruation and offer access to menstrual products and services, a number of projects have been developed. In India, however, more work has to be done to eliminate the stigma associated with menstruation and advance gender equality.

References

Anand, T., & Garg, S. (2015). Menstruation related myths in India: Strategies for combating it. Journal of Family Medicine and Primary Care, 4(2), 184. https://doi.org/10.4103/2249-4863.154627

Dr Kay standing., & Bee Hughes. (2019, May 28). How cultural attitudes to menstruation have finally started to shift. The British Academy. https://www.thebritishacademy.ac.uk/blog/summer-showcase-2019-how-cultural-attitudes-menstruation-have-finally-started-shift/

Guterman, M. A., Mehta, P., & Gibbs, M. S. (2007, December 31). Menstrual taboos among major religions.

Health & Family Welfare-Government of India, M. O. (n.d.). Menstrual Hygiene Scheme(MHS) :: National Health Mission. Menstrual Hygiene Scheme(MHS) :: National Health Mission. https://nhm.gov.in/index1.php?lang=1&level=3&sublinkid=1021&lid=391

Maharaj, T., & Winkler, I. T. (2020, July 25). Transnational Engagements: Cultural and Religious Practices Related to Menstruation. Transnational Engagements: Cultural and Religious Practices Related to Menstruation. https://doi.org/10.1007/978-981-15-0614-7_15

Menstruation Around the World – Your Period. (n.d.). Menstruation Around the World – Your Period. https://www.yourperiod.ca/normal-periods/menstruation-around-the-world/

Singh, A., Chakrabarty, M., Singh, S., Chandra, R., Chowdhury, S., & Singh, A. (2022, November 19). Menstrual hygiene practices among adolescent women in rural India: a cross-sectional study - BMC Public Health. BioMed Central. https://doi.org/10.1186/s12889-022-14622-7

CHAPTER NINE

Threads of Identity: Cross-Cultural Fashion and Social Identity

- Nirmitha Vuppalapati

Background

Understanding cross-cultural fashion differences among young Indian adults is critical for a variety of reasons. Knowing how fashion affects social identity is essential in today's more interconnected and globalized society. Fashion is a form of expression that represents one's cultural background, values, and beliefs. It is more than just clothes. Examining how Indian young adults use fashion to negotiate their social identities might provide important new perspectives on the complexities of inclusivity and cultural diversity.

Moreover, studying cross-cultural differences in fashion can help bridge gaps between communities and promote cultural understanding. Fashion serves as a visual language that extends beyond verbal communication, making it a powerful tool for fostering intercultural dialogue and appreciation. By exploring how individuals from diverse cultural backgrounds interpret and engage with fashion, we can foster respect for cultural differences and celebrate the richness of cultural diversity. It can also provide insight into how external factors, including globalization and social media, affect young Indian fashion choices. Gaining insight into how these elements influence personal tastes and fashion trends can help the fashion industry create more inclusive and culturally sensitive approaches.

In general, the research conducted on the fashion preferences of Indian young adults across cultural boundaries is noteworthy from both an academic and social standpoint. It could encourage inclusivity, raise cultural awareness, and foster a greater understanding of how fashion shapes social identities.

Fashion and Socio-cultural Factors

Fashion has been an integral part of human society for centuries. It not only reflects an individual's personal style but also serves as a means of social communication. The clothes people wear are often indicative of their cultural background, social status, and personality traits. As such, fashion has become an important aspect of social identity across cultures. However, the way people perceive and engage with fashion can vary significantly across cultures, making it an interesting topic for qualitative research. This paper aims to explore cross-cultural differences in fashion and their significance in social identity.

Social identity theory posits that an individual's self-concept is influenced by their membership in various social groups, such as ethnicity, nationality, gender, and age (Tajfel &Turner, 1979). People tend to conform to the norms and values of their social groups to establish a sense of belonging and a positive social identity. Fashion can play a crucial role in this process. For instance, certain dress codes are associated with specific social groups and can serve as a way of identifying oneself as a member of that group (e.g., wearing traditional clothing during cultural festivals).

However, the relationship between fashion and social identity is not universal. Different cultures have different norms and values regarding fashion, and these differences can have a significant impact on the way people use fashion to construct their social identity. For example, in some cultures, modesty is highly valued, and people tend to dress conservatively to avoid drawing attention to themselves. In contrast, other cultures may prioritise individual expression and encourage people to experiment with their clothing styles.

The significance of fashion in social identity can also vary depending on an individual's age, gender, and socioeconomic status. For example, young people may be more likely to use fashion to establish their social identity, whereas older people may be less concerned with fashion and more focused on other aspects of their identity, such as their professional achievements. Similarly, people from lower socioeconomic backgrounds may have limited access to fashionable clothing, whereas those from higher socioeconomic backgrounds may use fashion to signal their wealth and social status.

The cultural differences in fashion and their significance in social identity have important implications for the fashion industry and intercultural communication. For example, global fashion brands must be aware of cultural differences in fashion to effectively market their products across different cultures. Additionally, individuals from different cultures may interpret fashion cues differently, leading to misunderstandings and miscommunications. For instance, what may be considered a fashionable and appropriate outfit in one culture may be seen as inappropriate and offensive in another culture.

Despite the importance of cross-cultural differences in fashion and their significance in social identity, there is a limited amount of qualitative research on this topic. Most existing studies have focused on quantitative measures, such as surveys and experiments, to explore the relationship between fashion and social identity. However, qualitative research methods, such as interviews and observations, can provide a more in-depth understanding of the subjective experiences and meanings attached to fashion in different cultures.

Therefore, research was carried out to fill this gap by conducting a qualitative study to explore cross- cultural differences in fashion and their significance in social identity. Specifically, the study focused on 18 - 25-year-old young adults who are affiliated to different cultural groups within India. They were chosen because they represent a wide range of fashion norms and values, and the influence of outside cultures. By exploring the cultural differences in fashion and their significance in social identity, this paper sought to provide insights into the subjective experiences and meanings attached to fashion within and across cultures. The findings of this study can inform the fashion industry and intercultural communication and contribute to a better understanding of the role of fashion in social identity and promote inclusivity of diverse cultures.

Several studies have investigated the relationship between fashion and social identity. One study by Dittmar, Halliwell, and Ive (2006) explored how fashion preferences vary across cultures and how these preferences reflect an individual's social identity. The study found that individuals from different cultural backgrounds have distinct fashion preferences and that these preferences reflect their cultural values.

For instance, one of the most significant cross-cultural differences in fashion is the use of colour. In many Western cultures, black is considered a formal and sophisticated colour, while in many Asian cultures, it is associated with mourning and sadness (Choi, Lee, & Kim, 2017).

Similarly, red is considered a lucky and auspicious colour in many Asian cultures, while in Western cultures, it is often associated with passion and danger (Choi et al., 2017). A different significant cross-cultural difference in fashion is the use of fabric. In many African cultures, bright and colourful fabrics are popular, while in Western cultures, neutral colours and subdued patterns are more common (Kübler, 2017). Moreover, the use of specific fabrics such as silk, linen, or wool can also vary across cultures and regions.

Style is another aspect of fashion that can vary significantly across cultures. For example, traditional Japanese clothing such as the kimono is characterised by a loose fit, long sleeves, and a straight cut, while Western clothing tends to be more form-fitting and emphasises body shape (Kawamura, 2011). Similarly, Islamic clothing such as the hijab or abaya is characterised by modesty and covering the body, while Western clothing often emphasises revealing and exposing the body (Kawamura, 2011).

Another study by Kwon and Lennon (2009) examined the relationship between cultural values and fashion consumption among Korean and American college students. The study found that Korean students were more likely to value collectivism, whereas American students valued individualism. These values were reflected in their fashion choices, with Korean students more likely to prefer modest and conservative clothing styles, while American students preferred more provocative styles.

A study by Kim and Johnson (2016) explored how consumers from different cultures perceive luxury fashion brands. The study found that consumers from collectivist cultures valued the symbolic meaning of luxury brands more than consumers from individualistic cultures. Collectivist cultures valued luxury brands as a means of social status and belonging, whereas individualistic cultures valued luxury brands as a means of personal expression and uniqueness.

One of the ways cross-cultural differences in fashion affect social identity is by reinforcing cultural boundaries. Different fashion styles can indicate membership in a particular cultural group, which can lead to the creation of in-groups and out-groups (Kübler, 2017). For example, wearing traditional African clothing can indicate membership in a specific ethnic group, which can lead to a sense of belonging and solidarity among members of that group. Conversely, individuals who do not wear traditional African clothing may be perceived as outsiders or less connected to that cultural group.

Fashion can also serve as a way to resist cultural assimilation and maintain cultural identity. In many immigrant communities, fashion can serve as a way to preserve cultural traditions and practices (Kübler, 2017). For example, wearing traditional clothing can be a way to celebrate cultural heritage and resist pressure to assimilate into the dominant culture, and also be used as a way to challenge dominant cultural norms and values.

Therefore, cross-cultural differences in fashion reflect differences in cultural and social identity. These differences can be observed in various aspects of fashion, including colour, fabric, style, and patterns. Fashion can serve as a marker of social identity by reinforcing or even bridging the cultural boundaries. Cultural values, such as individualism and collectivism, influence fashion preferences and consumption patterns. Fashion can reveal significant insights into the social identity of individuals from different cultural backgrounds, highlighting the importance of understanding cross-cultural differences in fashion. Further research on this topic can help to deepen our understanding of the role of fashion in social identity and provide insights into the ways in which fashion can shape cultural practices and values.

Conclusion

The study on cross-cultural differences in fashion among Indian young adults aimed to explore the complex interplay between fashion, social identity, and cultural diversity. Through qualitative research with 20 participants from various Indian cultural backgrounds, the study explored the ways in which young adults use fashion as a means of social communication, cultural representation, and self-expression. The participants discussed how traditional Indian clothing is combining elements of Western design, emphasizing how their own style preferences are changing and how social media and globalization have affected their wardrobe choices. The study revealed the dynamic nature of fashion as a reflection of personal identity and cultural heritage, showcasing the intricate balance between traditional and modern elements in the participants' fashion choices.

In addition, the research yielded significant discoveries concerning the obstacles and opportunities posed by cultural differences in fashion for young adults from India. Cultural differences have occasionally caused misunderstandings and conflicts, but they have also served as inspiration for the development of fresh fashion trends that incorporate a variety of cultural elements. One noteworthy tendency among the participants was the incorporation of Western fashion styles, suggesting a move towards a more inclusive and worldwide fashion landscape. The way in which the participants reflected upon evolving notions of modesty and fashion acceptability highlighted the ways in which globalization and internet media have revolutionized fashion norms and values among young Indians.

However, it is essential to acknowledge the limitations of the study, such as the small sample size and the focus on a specific age group, which may limit the generalizability of the findings. The exclusion of individuals from low socioeconomic backgrounds and those residing outside India further limited the diversity of perspectives represented in the study. These drawbacks highlight the necessity for more comprehensive and diverse samples in future studies in order to fully capture the range of cross-cultural variations in Indian youth social identity and fashion. Despite these limitations, the study's ramifications go beyond academic research to influence business operations, governmental choices, and society's perceptions of fashion and ethnic diversity. By recognizing the significance of cross-cultural differences in fashion and social identity, stakeholders can promote a more inclusive and culturally sensitive approach to fashion design, marketing, and representation.

In conclusion, the study on cross-cultural differences in fashion among Indian young adults serves as a foundational exploration of the diverse sartorial landscapes that define contemporary Indian youth culture. Fashion serves as a bridge to link individuals across cultural borders, and the study promotes a more lively and peaceful society by embracing cultural diversity, fostering inclusivity, and honouring unique expressions through fashion. The insights gained from this study pave the way for future research to delve deeper into the complex dynamics of cross-cultural fashion, contributing to a more comprehensive understanding of the role of fashion in shaping social identities among Indian youth.

References

Tajfel, H., & Turner, J. C. (1979). An integrative theory of intergroup conflict. In W. G. Austin & S. Worchel (Eds.), The social psychology of intergroup relations (pp. 33-47). Monterey, CA: Brooks/Cole.

Tajfel, H., & Turner, J. C. (1986). The social identity theory of intergroup behavior. Psychology of Intergroup Relations, 7(1), 7-24.

Dittmar, H., Halliwell, E., & Ive, S. (2006). Does Barbie make girls want to be thin? The effect of experimental exposure to images of dolls on the body image of 5- to 8-year-old girls. Developmental Psychology, 42(2), 283-292.

Kwon, Y. J., & Lennon, S. J. (2009). Apparel consumption behaviour across two cultures: A comparative study of Korean and American college students. Clothing and Textiles Research Journal, 27(4), 271-285.

Mears, A., & Suri, S. (2010). Fashioning a National Identity: Indian Fashion and the Politics of Globalization. In S. Martens & A. Scott (Eds.), Fashioning Globalisation:

New Zealand Design, Working Women, and the Cultural Economy (pp. 231-247). Otago University Press.

Kawamura, Y. (2011). Fashion-ology: An introduction to fashion studies. Berg.

Kim, A. J., & Johnson, K. K. (2016). Cultural differences in luxury fashion branding: A comparison of Korean and US consumers' perceptions. Journal of Fashion Marketing and Management, 20(3), 292-307.

Choi, J., Lee, J., & Kim, H. (2017). Color meanings and cultural differences in color perception. Journal of Graphic Engineering and Design, 7(3), 87-97.

Kübler, J. (2017). Fashion and cultural studies. Routledge.

Pant, M. (2019, January 31). Fashion and Class: What Clothes Reveal About India's Social Structure. The Diplomat. https://thediplomat.com/2019/01/fashion-and-class-what-clothes- reveal-about-indias-social-structure/

CHAPTER TEN

Little Minds, Big Values: Children's Perception of Wealth

- **Prachi Aiyyappa K**

Background

Recognizing how children perceive wealth is critical to understanding the development of their financial views and behaviours. While much study has been done on adults' perceptions of wealth, there is a noteworthy gap in the literature about children's perspectives, particularly when comparing those from diverse familial backgrounds, such as children with parents and orphans. Previous research on children's understanding of wealth has mostly employed quantitative methods, examining characteristics such as allowance management, spending habits, and saving behaviours. These studies frequently emphasize the effect of parental supervision and socioeconomic position on children's financial literacy. Furnham (1999) found that children with financial competent parents are more likely to adopt good financial habits early on. However, there is insufficient qualitative study on children's complex views and attitudes about money. Qualitative approaches, such as interviews, can give more information about how children perceive wealth, what they value, and how their family circumstances impact these perceptions.

This study aims to address a gap in qualitative research on children's perceptions of wealth by contrasting the perspectives of children with parents with those of orphans. Understanding these differences and similarities can help to shape policies and educational programmes targeted at boosting financial literacy in children from varied backgrounds. Despite the broad recognition of the need of early financial education, little is known about how children from various household structures' view money. Existing research tends to generalize children's financial impressions without taking into account the specific experiences of orphans, who may not get direct parental financial assistance. Identifying common themes and differences in how children from these two groups define and value wealth, as well as understanding the impact of family structure on children's financial attitudes and beliefs, would provide insights on understanding the children better and also, on how to enhance financial literacy education for all children, regardless of their family situations.

Hence, this research aims to shed some light on the varying perspectives of wealth among children from different familial origins, by using qualitative interviews to create a more comprehensive picture in order to meet the requirements of children, ensuring they grow up with a thorough awareness of wealth and financial responsibility.

Children's perceptions of wealth often differ significantly from those of adults, according to developmental stages, social factors, and cognitive capacities. While adults define wealth in terms of financial stability, assets, and future security, children's perspectives are more immediate and flexible, shaped by their firsthand experiences and the socio-cultural framework in which they are raised. These differences in perception are rooted in cognitive development. Children's cognitive abilities are still growing, which limits their comprehension of abstract ideas like long-term financial planning and investing. According to Jean Piaget's theory of cognitive development, children in the preoperational stage (ages 2-7) are more focused on immediate, tangible experiences, and struggle to understand abstract ideas. As they become older and enter the concrete operational stage (ages 7-11), they learn more sophisticated ideas, but their impression of wealth is still heavily impacted by immediate and apparent variables (Piaget, 1952). Socio-cultural factors influence people's views of wealth. Children's perspectives are greatly shaped by their family environment, peers, and cultural narratives. For example, children from wealthy homes may have a different impression of wealth than those from less fortunate ones. Furthermore, cultural differences can influence how money is viewed and appreciated, with some cultures emphasizing community wealth and others focusing on individual gain.

Children's perception of wealth differs significantly depending on their family situation, particularly whether they have parents or are orphans. This disparity influences not just their immediate financial demands, but also their emotional and psychological perceptions of security, stability, and future prospects. According to research, children's views of wealth are strongly impacted by their home environment, caregivers' relationship, and the support networks accessible to them (Bowlby, 1982).

Children raised in stable, supportive households tend to view wealth through the perspective of emotional stability, consistent caring, and access to resources that meet their developmental requirements. Parental guidance and financial stability lay the groundwork for children to comprehend the larger consequences of wealth beyond tangible goods, instilling a feeling of security and confidence in their future. In contrast, orphaned children frequently experience a totally different view of wealth, marked by instability and worry about their future. Their perception of wealth may be based on survival necessities, safety, preparation for their future. They may lack stable caregiving interactions, which might damage their emotional resilience and capacity to create solid attachments that are critical for their development. The attachment theory states that stables bonds with caregivers (usually parents) are crucial to children's emotional well-being and capacity to handle relationships and problems in adulthood. Orphaned children may encounter difficulties in building these stable bonds, affecting their general development and perception of wealth (Bretherton, 1992). The socioeconomic context greatly impacts the children's perception of wealth. Orphaned children are generally economically disadvantaged and have restricted access to educational and developmental opportunities as compared to children with families. This disparity can in turn impact their attitudes towards social mobility and economic stability.

Review of Literature

Several studies and theoretical frameworks have been introduced and research upon to be able to explain the understanding of concepts like wealth and poverty among children. The social learning theory, by Albert Bandura, proposes that children acquire behaviours and attitudes through observation, imitation, and modelling. In the context of wealth perception, children watch and mimic their parents' financial behaviours and attitudes. Orphan children look up to the carers or role models whom they find binding (Bandura, 1977). We also have Jean Piaget's cognitive development theory, which states that children's understanding of abstract concepts like wealth in this case, develop as they progress through various cognitive developmental stages. Progressing into the intricate factors that revolve around this study, we have socioeconomic status as one of the highlighted factors in most studies. Socioeconomic status impacts children's cognitive and emotional development. Children from better socioeconomic families frequently have greater access to resources, which might influence their perceptions of wealth. On the other hand, children from lower socioeconomic backgrounds, or orphans, may have different perspectives and views as a result of their experiences with economic scarcity (Bradley & Corwyn, 2002). Leon Festinger's social comparison theory states that people establish their social and personal value by comparing themselves to others. Similarly, children too may compare their family's wealth to that of their peers, which in turn influences their perspective of their own financial situation. Orphaned children may compare their circumstances to that of children with parents, or the outside world that they interact with on a daily basis, influencing their self-perception and concept of wealth and riches (Festinger, 1954). The importance of ecological systems under a topic like this has been explained by Urie Bronfenbrenner's ecological systems theory. The theory emphasizes on the several layers of the environment that impact a child's development, such as their family, school, community, and social factors. This helps in contributing to a better understanding of how diverse circumstances influence children's perception of wealth.

Children's perception of wealth is strongly impacted by their immediate family surroundings and interactions with their parents. Parents are the primary agents of financial socialization, instilling information and attitudes about money in their children. They affect their children's perceptions through direct instruction, behaviour modelling, and financial discussions. According to research, children who engage in financial discussions, with their parents have a more comprehensive knowledge of economic concepts and are better at money management (Gudmunson & Danes, 2011). Open and effective family communication about money can have a significant impact on children's financial literacy and views of wealth. Families that openly discuss budgeting, saving, and spending practices teach their children real money management skills and foster a healthy attitude towards money. This kind of transparency helps to develop reasonable expectations and needs along with a balanced perspective on wealth. Parental attitudes towards money and their financial behaviours serve as models for children. Habits like saving up, or on the contrary overspending, can influence and impact the children greatly. Emphasis of wealth at home, on what types and kinds of things, for example necessities like food, shelter, education or on the contrary shopping, materialistic things would be like setting an example for children, on the basis of which they would start building a foundation of where money stands for them, what it actually means, and where they should put it to use. This is where the influence of family lifestyle and consumption patterns come into picture. The family's lifestyle and consumption habits have a significant impact on children's perceptions of wealth. Families who prioritize luxury products and experiences may end up fostering the idea of wealth as the collection of high-status stuff. Families that emphasize frugality and satisfaction with basic requirements, may teach their children to view wealth as financial security and simple living (Morris, 2011). Cultural and societal norms regarding wealth and financial behaviour impact how youngsters view money in their family context. Cultural views towards money, work ethic, and social position influence the financial values passed down by parents to their offspring. Children in cultures that emphasize modesty and group well-being may perceive prosperity via community support and resource sharing. In more individualistic societies, wealth may be considered as a personal accomplishment and a route to individual independence.

Orphaned children frequently encounter unique problems that might significantly influence their perceptions of wealth. How these children comprehend and connect to wealth and poverty is influenced by a variety of elements, including their living environment, social relationships, and psychological well-being. Orphaned children commonly face emotional and psychological issues as a result of loss of parents and instability in their living arrangements. These experiences can have a tremendous impact on their impression of wealth. They might associate wealth with not just financial resources, but also emotional security, and stability which they frequently lack. The psychological effects of orphanhood might result in a greater awareness of economic scarcity and a more pragmatic view of wealth

(Whetten et al., 2011). The surroundings in which orphaned children are nurtured are critical to their economic and social development. Orphanages and foster homes frequently operate with little financial means, which might influence children's attitudes on wealth and resource management. Children might acquire a strong sense of resourcefulness and place a higher importance on tiny financial gains. The communal living setup in orphanages may also foster a collective approach to resources, influencing their perception of wealth as shared rather than individualistic. Orphaned children often compare their situations to those of their non-orphaned peers, which influences their perception of wealth. These comparisons might evoke feelings of inadequacy or resentment, particularly when there is a notable disparity in material assets and possibilities. Such comparisons highlight the social dimension of wealth, where it is not seen in absolute terms, but in relation to one's immediate social environment (Festinger, 1954). Despite the difficulties, many orphaned children acquire strong coping strategies and resilience, which shape their view of wealth. They place a higher emphasis on non-material dimensions of wealth, such as education, connections, and personal accomplishments. Resilience can lead to a more balanced and comprehensive understanding of wealth, in which economic status is simply one of the many factors that influence overall well-being (Masten & Narayan, 2012).

Findings and Discussion

The interview was conducted among two distinct groups of children. It included a 20-person sample, where 10 children were orphans and the other 10 were children with parents. The participants that participated in the research were between nine to twelve years of age. After systematically reviewing the data in order to identify themes, patterns, and relationships that emerge from the participants' responses, a set of common and different themes was identified, which helped in providing a rich and detailed understanding of the topic.

Talking about the common themes that were found, personal qualities were the most talked about. Orphans often valued personal qualities over material wealth, with one stating, "I think being rich meant having a good heart, good qualities, and someone whose behaviours are perceived to be nice." This suggests orphans see wealth as a source of happiness, emphasizing traits like adaptability, independence, and emotional strength due to their lack of parental guidance. Similarly, some children with parents also valued personal qualities over financial wealth, with one mentioning, "Rich for me is having a happy and fulfilling life, that includes good health and good relationships." For these children, qualities like resilience, self-discipline, and a positive attitude were important, especially if they came from disadvantaged backgrounds. Secondly, the value of hard work was often emphasized in the discussions while the children were answering both in terms of orphans and children with parents. "When people work and stand on their own feet and do something all by themselves with their efforts and hard work that is when I think thought a person could earn money." As said by one of the orphan subjects, they emphasize the need for them to work hard in order to achieve anything in their life, or be wealthy. For them, the value of hard work might be very important in particular as they often have to solely rely on their own efforts and resources to succeed and come up in life. As thought before taking the interviews, it was perceived that children with parents would not lean on the factor of hard work as much as the orphans would, but the interviews said otherwise. As said by one of the subjects with parents "Ah, only by working hard one can earn money? I mean there are other ways but hard work is the best." For these children, the examples set by their parent's hard work and dedication toward their careers or business may influence their own attitude towards work and success. The dimension of social responsibility was almost emphasized just as much as hard work.

The value of social responsibility was seen in both orphans and children with parents equally, which was very surprising as it was not expected. "I want to be able to give other orphans like me the facilities that I am receiving as I feel that there are a lot of them out there that are not being treated well." The following was said by an orphan, someone that has experienced hardship and adversity, social responsibility may be particularly important as they may have a greater appreciation for the importance of supporting others and giving back to those in need. As said by a child with parents "I want to help old people at old-age homes, I have grandparents at home and ajji is very caring and so I think everyone at the old-age home is too. I will put the money there and make them have a good time so that they are never sad". It is seen that they equally place importance on giving back to society. They may believe that those who have accumulated wealth have a greater responsibility to give back to their communities and contribute to the greater good. It might be possible that they have instilled values of social responsibility in them and may also prioritize making a positive impact in communities and beyond. Multidimensional wealth, the concept of wealth as encompassing more than just financial or material resources. It recognizes that individuals and communities have diverse and complex needs and values, and that wealth can take many forms beyond monetary assets. This dimension, a complicated one at that, was surprisingly common in both the groups of children as well. As said by one of the subjects "Anyone who has money is rich but also someone that has a good heart. Only money isn't enough, but also someone who works hard is rich I feel". For them, their well-being and quality of life are impacted by more than just financial resources, and factors such as human and social capital, natural resources, and cultural heritages can also play a significant role in their overall sense of wealth and prosperity. One of the subjects with parents also said ". I think that anyone that does hard work and has good qualities and someone who earns money is truly rich, for example, labourers that work for the whole day without complaining" they recognized that wealth is not just about accumulating financial resources, but also about investing in human and social capital, natural resources, and cultural heritage, they can gain a greater appreciation for the diverse and complex factors that contribute to their well-being and success. Lastly, a dimension that was completely out of the blue, that would not have been expected to be talked about, power dynamics, was brought into picture by these children. Power can be defined as the ability to influence or control the behaviour of others, and power dynamics can be seen in the ways in which power is distributed among individuals or groups and how it is exercised in different situations. It is also a key aspect of social and organizational life, shaping relationships and interactions between individuals and groups and influencing how resources and opportunities are distributed within a particular context. As said by an orphan and a child with parents respectively

"Poor people are those that are always in difficulty, someone that works under rich people" and "I don't know (pauses) I think the only differences is that rich people have access to better education and hospital facilities than poor people, that is why poor people work for the rich" both these responses show the power dynamic value of the children from both the categories which indicate that both the categories think that poor people are very inferior to the rich and that they always have to work under the rich in order to gain wealth/earn money.

Conclusion

The analysis of the responses received proved that yes orphans do perceive wealth to be different, but on the larger picture, it was noticed that for the age groups of nine to twelve most of the children had the similar kind of thought process when it came to perceiving wealth. Yes, there were differences between the two groups as seen in various answers, but it could be noticed that many more responses showed the children having the same perception of wealth.

The perception of wealth between orphans and children with parents could be seen varying depending upon a variety of factors like, cultural and socioeconomic backgrounds. However, in general, it can be said that children with parents may have a more stable and consistent perception of wealth compared to orphans. They may also have access to resources and opportunities to increase their wealth and financial literacy exposure. On the other hand, orphans may have a more fluid and uncertain perception of wealth, as they may lack the stability and guidance. They might also be more acutely aware of the disparities between their own circumstances and those of others around them, which can impact their perception of wealth. It was also observed that children with parents have various perspectives about wealth in general compared to orphans who see money as a need to grow and not necessarily as a want. To conclude, it can be said that orphans perceive wealth as a source of privilege, entitlement, and happiness while children with parents perceive wealth as a status symbol and a means to achieve success and succeed in life majorly.

References

Bowlby, J. (1982). Attachment and Loss (Vol. 1). Hogarth Press.

Bretherton, I. (1992). The origins of attachment theory: John Bowlby and Mary Ainsworth. Developmental Psychology, 28(5), 759–775. https://doi.org/10.1037/0012-1649.28.5.759

Festinger, L. (1954). A theory of social comparison processes. Human Relations, 7(2), 117–140. https://doi.org/10.1177/001872675400700202

Furnham, A. (1999). The saving and spending habits of young people. Journal of Economic Psychology, 20(6), 677–697. https://doi.org/10.1016/s0167-4870(99)00030-6

Gudmunson, C. G., & Danes, S. M. (2011). Family Financial Socialization: Theory and Critical review. Journal of Family and Economic Issues, 32(4), 644–667. https://doi.org/10.1007/s10834-011-9275-y

Mary D. Salter Ainsworth, Mary C. Blehar, Everett Waters, and Sally Wall. Hillsdale, N.J., Erlbaum, (1978). Patterns of attachment: A psychological study of the strange situation. ResearchGate.

Masten, A. S., & Narayan, A. J. (2012). Child Development in the context of Disaster, war, and Terrorism: Pathways of risk and resilience. Annual Review of Psychology, 63(1), 227–257. https://doi.org/10.1146/annurev-psych-120710-100356

Morris, E. (2011). Book Review: Longing and Belonging: Parents, Children and Consumer Culture. By Allison J. Pugh. Berkeley: University of California Press, 2009. Gender & Society, 25(1), 129–131. https://doi.org/10.1177/0891243210387596

Piaget, J. (1952). The origins of intelligence in children. W W Norton & Co. https://doi.org/10.1037/11494-000

Piaget, J. (1971). the theory of stages in cognitive development. in D. Green, M. P. Ford, & G. B. Flamer (eds.), measurement and Piaget (pp. 1-11). New York, NY McGraw-Hill. - references - scientific research publishing. (n.d.). https://www.scirp.org/reference/referencespapers?referenceid=2277292

Whetten, K., Ostermann, J., Whetten, R., O'Donnell, K., & Thielman, N. (2011). More than the loss of a parent: Potentially traumatic events among orphaned and abandoned children. Journal of Traumatic Stress, 24(2), 174–182. https://doi.org/10.1002/jts.20625

CHAPTER ELEVEN

Digital Marketplace: Cultural Insights from Online Shoppers

- **Aparna Swamy**

Background

The importance of online buying is increasing worldwide, and culture has a big impact on consumer behaviour, which makes this study on how Indian students' online purchasing habits are affected by it necessary. Understanding the cultural quirks that influence online purchasing behaviours is essential for companies looking to improve customer experiences and create marketing strategies that work as online shopping grows in popularity. This study examines how intercultural exposure, perceived dangers, and economic and psychological aspects affect Indian students' decisions to shop online. Indian students represent a significant portion of the market, which is growing quickly. The research helps businesses create more welcoming and inclusive online shopping experiences by addressing these elements and providing insightful information to the disciplines of consumer behaviour and cross-cultural psychology.

The significance of studying online shopping behaviour has grown with the global expansion of digital commerce. The development of the internet and other cutting-edge technologies has fundamentally altered consumer buying behaviour by enabling people to buy goods and services from the comfort of their homes. Numerous elements, including cultural features that are vital in forming people's attitudes and views regarding internet purchasing, have an impact on this shift in consumer behaviour.

Culture is the shared beliefs, morals, customs, behaviours, and artefacts of a group or civilization (Matsumoto & Juang, 2016). It addresses many different subjects, such as language, religion, education, social structure, and technology, among others. Since culture influences people's feelings, thoughts, and behaviours, it is a crucial concept in psychology. Culture affects people's mental processes, socialisation strategies, emotional expressions, and communication styles, among other psychological phenomena (Henrich et al., 2010).

One of the main theories explaining how culture affects psychological processes is the socio-cultural approach. This theory holds that cultural factors shape society norms, expectations, and models that affect people's attitudes, behaviours, and emotions, hence influencing human growth and functioning (Vygotsky, 1978). An additional relevant perspective is provided by the cross-cultural psychology technique, which studies the similarities and differences in human conduct across cultural boundaries. This field seeks to identify psychological processes that are common to all humans as well as culturally differentiated processes unique to specific civilizations (Matsumoto & Juang, 2016).

Culture is a complex, diverse concept that has a significant impact on people's mental health. Understanding how culture influences people's emotions, behaviour, and thought processes is essential to developing intercultural understanding and developing successful treatments. Online purchasing behaviour refers to the attitudes, opinions, intentions, and actions that people exhibit when they make purchases online (Bhatnagar, Misra, & Rao, 2000). It covers a wide range of topics, such as product descriptions, payment options, shipping options, and customer assistance in addition to website design Online purchase behaviour has been studied using a variety of psychological approaches, including consumer behaviour, social psychology, and cognitive psychology.

Researchers have discovered that a variety of factors, including personal characteristics, environmental factors, and website elements, have an impact on how customers behave when making purchases online (Donthu & Garcia, 1999; Gefen, Karahanna, & Straub, 2003). One important theoretical framework for understanding online buying behaviour is the Technology Acceptance Model (TAM). This idea holds that people's intentions to utilise technology depend on how useful and easy they perceive it to be (Davis, 1989). Several studies that have utilised this model to study online buying behaviour have found that perceived utility, usability, and trust are significant predictors of online purchase intentions (Lee & Park, 2009; Venkatesh & Davis, 2000).

Another relevant point of view is the social influence hypothesis, which maintains that people's behaviour is influenced by group norms and social pressure (Cialdini & Goldstein, 2004). When this theory is applied to online buying behaviour, social influence elements—like social media, peer recommendations, and online reviews—have been shown to significantly influence customers' purchasing decisions (Cheung & Lee, 2010; Huang, Huang, & Wu, 2016).

Review of Literature

The study "Understanding Online Purchase Intentions: Contributions from Technology and Trust Perspectives," by Chen and Barnes (2011), focuses on the influence of technology and trust while examining the factors that influence customers' inclinations to make online purchases of items. According to the writers, two important aspects that influence a person's decision to make an online purchase are trust and technology. They argue that customers' perceptions of a website's usability, usefulness, and technical quality affect their purchasing decisions. Customers' confidence in the website's privacy and security features also affects their purchasing intentions. A survey was utilised in the study to collect data from 304 Taiwanese clients. The findings show that although customers' intentions to make a purchase are positively impacted by their perceptions of the website's usability and technical superiority, perceived value has no discernible effect. Furthermore, customers' intentions to make purchases are positively impacted by their level of trust in the website, especially with regard to its security and privacy aspects. The study also found that age and gender mitigate the relationship between technology, traits related to trust, and inclinations to buy. The study's findings contribute to our understanding of consumers' intentions to make online purchases and offer guidance to marketers and online retailers on how to improve the functionality and dependability of their websites to enhance consumer buy intentions.

The study "Factors Influencing Online Shopping Behaviour: The Mediating Role of Purchase Intention" by Lim et al. (2017) investigates the variables influencing consumers' online shopping behaviour by looking at the mediating role of buy intention. The study's objective is to understand the relationships between the numerous factors that affect consumers' intent to buy and their online buying behaviour. The authors claim that purchase intention plays a major mediating role in the relationship between the factors influencing online buying behaviour, such as perceived utility, perceived ease of use, perceived enjoyment, perceived risk, and trust. In order to test the components and collect data from 316 Malaysian internet users, a structured questionnaire was employed in the study. The findings show that while perceived usefulness, perceived ease of use, and perceived enjoyment have positive effects on purchase intention, perceived danger has a negative effect. Furthermore, the intention to buy influences online activity in a positive way. The study also found that trust plays a major mediating role in the relationship between perceived risk and purchase intention. The study's conclusions contribute to our understanding of how factors like purchasing intention influence consumers' online purchasing behaviour. The authors suggest that online retailers focus on developing websites that are useful, easy to use, and enjoyable in order to enhance consumers' purchase intent and online shopping habit.

The study "An Analysis of Factors Affecting on Consumers' Online Shopping Behaviour" by Javadi et al. (2012) examines the factors influencing consumers' online purchasing behaviour. The study's objective is to identify the critical factors that influence both the real online purchasing behaviour of consumers and their buying intentions. The authors propose that the factors impacting online purchase behaviour can be broadly classified into three categories: environmental factors, website factors, and individual factors. Individual variables include things like age, gender, income, and level of education. Aspects of a website include those that are directly related to it, like dependability, security, and usability. Examples of environmental factors are societal and cultural norms, trust, and legal constraints.

To evaluate the constructs and gather data from 384 Iranian internet shoppers, a structured questionnaire was employed. The research indicates that factors such as website design, website security, and website trust have a significant impact on the online buying behaviour of customers. Personal attributes such as age and educational attainment can influence online shopping behaviours. The study's conclusions assist online retailers and marketers in better understanding the factors influencing consumers' online buying decisions and in developing strategies that will enhance their clients' online shopping encounters. The factors influencing Indian urban customers' online purchasing behaviour are examined by the author of the essay "Factors Influencing Online Purchasing Behaviour of Urban Consumers in India" (Nittala, 2015).

The author argues that a number of variables, such as personal traits, contextual circumstances, and website-related factors, influence what people buy online. Personal factors encompass demographic elements like age, gender, income, education, and job. Situational concerns include things like convenience, time constraints, and customer needs. A website's usability, security, and trustworthiness are examples of website-related variables. A methodical survey was employed to gather information from 200 internet users in Hyderabad, India, and assess the frameworks. The findings show that personal attributes like money, age, and gender have a big impact on consumers' online purchasing decisions. Convenience and the customer's need for the items are examples of situational factors that influence online buying behaviour. The survey also discovered that aspects of websites, such security and appearance, have a big influence on how people purchase online.

The study's findings highlight the need of developing effective online marketing strategies in order to enhance customers' online buying experiences and provide light on the factors impacting the online purchase behaviour of urban Indian consumers. "A Study of the Relationship between Shopping Orientation and Online Shopping Behaviour Among Indian Youth" (Handa and Gupta, 2015) examines the relationship between young Indians' online shopping behaviour and their shopping orientation. The study aims to identify the factors influencing the online purchasing behaviour of Indian adolescents and how shopping orientation fits into this context.

According to the authors, a significant determinant of online buying behaviour is shopping orientation, which characterises how people approach and feel about making purchases. 358 Indian teenagers between the ages of 18 and 25 participated in the study, and their online shopping habits and purchasing preferences were evaluated using a questionnaire. Five aspects of purchasing orientation—social, economic, convenient, recreational, and value orientation—as well as two variables of online shopping behavior—online search behaviour and online purchase behavior—are included in the questionnaire. he findings show that young Indians' online buying behaviour is highly influenced by their shopping orientation. Specifically, online search activity is significantly correlated with convenience orientation, while online shopping behaviour is positively correlated with social and recreational orientations. The study also found that young Indians' inclination to make online purchases is not considerably influenced by their economic or value orientations. The study's findings highlight the significance of understanding individual differences in shopping orientation in order to develop effective online marketing strategies and provide insight into how shopping orientation affects the online purchasing behaviour of young Indian customers.In their 2016 essay "An Analysis of Factors Affecting on Online Buying Behaviour of Customers," Nagra and Gopal examine the factors influencing the online purchasing habits of Indian customers.

The study aims to identify the critical factors influencing consumers' intentions to make purchases online as well as their actual online behaviour. The authors argue that a range of factors influence customers' online purchasing behaviour, including personal traits, aspects connected to websites, and factors related to trust. Individual variables include things like prior internet use, age, gender, income, and education. Usability, security, and website design are a few examples of components linked to webpages. Considerations pertaining to trust include things like perceived danger, confidence in the website, and confidence in the vendor.

To gather information and test the components, 200 Indian internet users answered a structured questionnaire. The findings show that individual factors like age, gender, and educational attainment have a big impact on consumers' decisions to make purchases online. The design, usability, and security of websites have considerable impact on consumers' online purchasing decisions. The study also found that customers' online purchasing behaviour was significantly influenced by factors related to trust, such as perceptions of risk and seller confidence. The study's findings highlight the significance of developing effective online marketing strategies in order to enhance customers' online shopping experiences and throw light on the factors influencing Indian consumers' online purchase behaviour.

The factors influencing Indian customers' online shopping decisions are examined by Sinha and Kim (2013) in their work "Factors impacting Indian consumers' online buying behaviour". The goal of the study is to identify the key factors influencing the online buying decisions and behaviours of Indian consumers. The authors argue that a variety of factors influence customers' online purchase decisions, including individual characteristics, factors connected to websites, and factors linked to products. Personal qualities include elements like age, income, gender, and level of education. Website characteristics include things like security, usability, and design. Product-related factors include things like product quality, cost, and brand reputation.

To gather information from 218 Indian online shoppers and test the constructs, a methodical questionnaire was employed. The findings show that Indian consumers' decisions to make online purchases are significantly influenced by personal factors like wealth and education. Online purchase decisions are also influenced by website-related factors like security and design. The survey also revealed that factors related to the products Indian consumers buy online, like brand reputation and product quality, had a big impact on their online buying habits. The study's findings highlight the significance of developing effective online marketing strategies that take these factors into account and throw light on the factors influencing Indian customers' decisions to buy products online.

Findings and Discussion

Three themes were found, that repeated among various students with multicultural and non-multicultural exposure. These results are specific to the 20 participants but gives an in-depth understanding of their behaviour with respect to Online shopping and cultural effect on online shopping behaviour. The main three themes that were recurring throughout the interview with 20 people were:

1. Perceived Risk
2. Product Risk
3. Price

Product Risk

One of the main reasons the subjects worried about product risk when they were shopping online was the lack of a physical inspection. When they shopped at physical locations, they noted that they could examine items in-person and assess their quality before making a purchase. Another factor that increases the risk of purchasing a fraudulent product when shopping online is its prevalence. In addition to being more difficult to distinguish from real goods, fake goods may also be of worse quality, which poses a risk.

Perceived Risk

Perceived risk is the term used to describe the subjective evaluation of likely negative consequences that may arise from a purchase decision. When it comes to internet shopping, perceived risk can involve concerns over the products' quality, the safety of one's money and personal information, and the vendor's reliability. One of the primary elements influencing the perception of internet purchases as dangerous is the absence of direct touch with the goods or vendor. The subjects expressed scepticism regarding the product's quality and the seller's trustworthiness. Additionally, they expressed concerns regarding the product's validity and the security of their financial and personal data.

Price

Price was a major factor affecting online shoppers' decisions. Due to the fact that participants were constantly looking for the greatest deal, price is a key consideration when making a purchase. Regarding price, respondents reported acting impulsively to purchase items even in times of financial hardship since they would later feel satisfied mentally. One of the main ways that pricing affected internet shoppers' activity was through comparison shopping. Because a variety of internet firms were easily accessible, subjects were able to evaluate pricing for the same or similar commodities across multiple websites.

Because price is often a deciding factor for consumers, respondents were able to pick the best offers. When there was a significant discount, subjects were more inclined to visit websites with the most alluring deals and spend more money—even if it was a sizable amount. Price reductions and promotional materials, such as promotions or coupon codes, were used to sway the subjects' decisions to make a purchase. Retailers may also use dynamic pricing strategies, which adjust prices in real-time in response to factors including demand, inventory levels, and competitors' prices, to attract customers and increase sales.

The price has an impact on consumers' perceptions of a product's value. People often associated higher prices with better quality, and if they thought a thing was worth more, they might be prepared to pay extra for it. In contrast, individuals were less inclined to purchase a product if they thought its price was too high in relation to its perceived value.

Conclusion

Online purchasing behaviour is a complex, multilayered construct that incorporates a range of psychological mechanisms. Companies that comprehend the factors influencing consumers' online purchasing behaviour can develop online platforms and marketing strategies that are more effective.

References

Bhatnagar, A., Misra, S., & Rao, H. R. (2000). On risk, convenience, and Internet shopping behavior. Communications of the ACM, 43(11), 98-105.

Cheung, C. M., & Lee, M. K. (2010). A theoretical model of intentional social action in online shopping. Decision Support Systems, 49(3), 246-254.

Cialdini, R. B., & Goldstein, N. J. (2004). Social influence: Compliance and conformity.

Annual Review of Psychology, 55, 591-621.

Davis, F. D. (1989). Perceived usefulness, perceived ease of use, and user acceptance of information technology. MIS Quarterly, 13(3), 319-340.

Donthu, N., & Garcia, A. (1999). The Internet shopper. Journal of Advertising Research, 39(3), 52-58.

Gefen, D., Karahanna, E., & Straub, D. W. (2003). Trust and TAM in online shopping: An integrated model. MIS Quarterly, 27(1), 51-90.

Henrich, J., Heine, S. J., & Norenzayan, A. (2010). The weirdest people in the world? Behavioral and Brain Sciences, 33(2-3), 61-83. https://doi.org/10.1017/S0140525X0999152X

Huang, Z., Huang, L., & Wu, Q. (2016). Social influence and consumer behavior in online shopping: Evidence from a panel study. Journal of Business Research, 69(7), 2614-2621.

Javadi, M. H. M., Dolatabadi, H. R., Nourbakhsh, M., Poursaeedi, A., & Asadollahi, A. R. (2012). An analysis of factors affecting on online shopping behavior of consumers. International Journal of Marketing Studies, 4(5), 81-98. https://doi.org/10.5539/ijms.v4n5p81

Lee, J., & Park, D. H. (2009). Understanding consumers' online shopping and purchasing behaviors. Journal of Retailing and Consumer Services, 16(5), 377-385.

Lim, Y. J., Osman, A., Salahuddin, S. N., & Romle, A. R. (2017). Factors influencing online shopping behavior: The mediating role of purchase intention. Procedia Computer Science, 124, 815-822. https://doi.org/10.1016/j.procs.2017.12.235

Matsumoto, D., & Juang, L. (2016). Culture and psychology. Nelson Education.

Nagra, G., & Gopal, R. (2016). An study of factors affecting on online shopping behavior of consumers. International Journal of Marketing and Technology, 6(1), 68-78. https://doi.org/10.11648/j.ijmt.2016.0601.11

Nittala, R. (2015). Factors influencing online shopping behavior of urban consumers in India. International Journal of Online Marketing, 5(1), 38-50. https://doi.org/10.4018/

IJOM.2015010103.

Sinha, J., & Kim, J. (2013). Factors affecting Indian consumers' online buying behavior. Journal of Retail

• 145 •

CHAPTER TWELVE

Love Across Borders: Complexities of Cross-Cultural Marriage

- **Sanjana Sakaray**

Background

Intercultural marriage is very common in a lot of countries and it is increasing a very steady pace. When talking about intercultural marriage, it is imperative to talk about culture first. Culture has a close connection to economic, social, and political establishments. Cultural and societal structures evolve together and interact. Culture plays a significant role in shaping social institutions. Types of social, economic and political arrangements are shaped by societal wealth, authority buildings, and perceived meanings. Culture shapes financial, political, family, and educational institutions, which in turn shape culture. Social institutions and culture interact mutually. The institution of family plays an essential part in human interactions. Through advancements in technology, increased international travel, and the shifting of economic centers, there has been a rise in cross-cultural interactions. Every partner brings in their personal history, educational background, and beliefs into their expectations for the relationship and its future. Even though there are many traditional beliefs and values that couples from the same culture share, there will still be significant differences in how each views the relationship. There can be significant differences in culture when a couple is from two different backgrounds. Intercultural marriages occur when people from different cultures decide to come together as a family after meeting. Even though there have been many examples of these cross-cultural unions in the past, the number of these unions is still rising globally. These unions provide people with multicultural life experiences.

There is mention of how cross culture marriage is across the world, what are its strengths and its downfalls. There is also mention of how some cultures differ in cross culture marriage and gender part and the aspects which are important for maintaining a steady relationship with the partner, in-laws and the extended family and how family resilience is important in a family. The term "culture" refers to a collection of mutual worldviews and adaptive actions that result from participation in a number of backgrounds at the same time, which includes environmental setting (rural, urban, suburban), religious background, nationality and ethnicity, social class, minority status, occupation, political position, migratory patterns, stage of acculturation, and standards resulting from sharing a generation, historical period, or specific ideology (Falicov, 1998). Cross culture marriage is a kind of marriage when two people from two different cultures marry each other; it becomes a cross culture marriage. There will be many difficulties to face when both the cultures are combines. There are 5 "Cs" which are the most crucial attributes which plays a part in lifelong marriage relationship satisfaction. The five "Cs" are commitment, caring, communication, conflict and compromise and contract which denotes to the marital partners' direct and indirect expectations of each other and their marriages" (Cheung, 2005). In the modern years intercultural wedding has turned into fashion of sort globally. Individuals are no longer cut off from their native environments and cultural traditions. People who married people from different culture are upholding their relationship with great understanding and broadmindedness for each other. According to Frame (2004), Over the last three decades there has been an unprecedented increase in interracial and intercultural marriage. One can disagree, though, and question if intercultural unions always benefit families and religion. Due to cultural differences, cross-cultural couples encounter several issues and tension practically daily in their lives. But, if the couple addresses communication skills and cultural differences, marriage can still succeed in spite of these difficulties. Intercultural marriages and their intimacy are clear and it is spreading in society throughout. Culture may comprise of their language, religion or ethnicity. Currently, America has one of the most diverse and multiracial cultures in the world. Though no one knows about this, in the 1966, 17 states of U.S had rules in contradiction of the intercultural and mixed race wedding. The state kept a check on marriages amongst whites and other races in the country. There is a lot of discrimination against children of different cultures. The nature of these relationships and marital satisfaction has only been studied empirically, despite the fact that there are a lot of international marriages in the United States today (Ngye and Snyder).

The style of communication and interactive relationship are essential characteristics of culture and it varies very theatrically from one culture to another. There will be obstacles in linguistic and communication. It is significant to keep in mind that everybody on earth has culture not just the populations that are regarded as "civilized". The bulk of culture exists under the surface, unnoticed. For instance, when a Russian man is married to an Italian woman, there are a number of cultural differences that come into play, including the ways in which people express their emotions, how they handle conflict, and how family origin is important in bringing up kids (Sullivan and Cotton, 2007). The most problematic to change when it is absolutely being the beliefs and the value which lie under the surface. The arrangement of two different cultures will have an outcome in a diversity of life experiences and opportunities, but there will be many major challenges coming along in their marriage. Adapting a new culture into their life and following its customs and traditions may not be as easy it seems. Even if marrying the person, your love can look like a romantic love story, the truth is that, adapting to new culture and the pressure given by the parents can be very infuriating and can be very challenging in real life experience.

Marriages between people of different races, religions, and ethnicities present exceptional occasions for meaningful and creative connections. Until now, if the worldviews of spouses are highly differing, there may be potential conflicts. There can be resilience from family, friends and societies. There may be major difference in values and rituals of the family origins. The "cultural outsider" may raise disapprovals from one or both family members. The new other half could go through "cultural shock" or feel uncomfortable around the other's relatives. The factors that determine whether a marriage will succeed or fail, be happy or not, are immensely complex and if it can simply be reduced to amounts of differences and similarities in culture. Cross-cultural marriages are immensely complex and diverse, which makes it extremely problematic to derive generalizations that the clinician may use without digging deeper into the linked family process.

Conceptualization of Marriage

Social psychologists provide two groups of theories where there is a link between marital love and cultural consonance or conflict. According to the idea of modern society, marriages must always be established on a sentimental foundation, or on the sense of shared love. One of the theories states that this type of love has a better chance at booming there love when they have the same similarities of background. The compatibility of social and cultural experiences significantly promotes the sensation of rapport, which is so essential for the development of love.

A significant groundwork for determining the range of individuals for whom one may have empathy is one's social and cultural background. One would be able to understand someone with a comparable religious and educational background and so increase the likelihood of developing rapport. These broad characteristics include religious upbringing and education background. According to Berman, theories that highlight the relevance of parallels for marital compatibility prefer to be gloomy about cross-cultural marriages and point to the high divorce rate as indications of the problems these marriages face.

According to Crohn, finding grounds of commonality between the potential couples is actually emphasized in the majority of interfaith couples counselling.

Another set of beliefs on love is based on the absolute reverse logic, highlighting the significance of diversity for achieving individual needs in a relationship. It's a common notion that "opposites attract" and work well with each other (Winch, 1955). Most of the early computerized dating systems were based on this notion of complementary psychological needs (Schulz, 1976). In agreement with psychodynamic authors, differences in culture are just abuses of power for the partner's complementing wants. The objective is to figure out whether the partnership offers the warmness, affection, love, excitement, care, intimacy, and solidarity that all people need. Behind the masks of two racially diverse persons, this is the qualification. Because "it takes two to tango," a person either intentionally or unintentionally chooses a partner who enhances a specific dance move or toad in life (Jester, 1982).

According to Falicov, there will be corresponding differences which are mentioned to be different in personality, though quite comparable disagreement can be used to find significance in cultural differences between partners. One such perspective would highlight the excellent options to spouses in intercultural marriages. For instance, a WASP man who is a workaholic, task-person is married to a woman from Latin culture and who is a hail-fellow-well-met kind of person. A deeper and more complete total might result by integrating these two contrasting backgrounds than if each member had humans someone from their own culture. According to Goldner (1982), cross-cultural couples could be seen as a new, more complex practice of marriage than the traditional consanguineous unions of traditional societies, according to a modern, optimistic view of intermarriage, which might also comprise of numerous classes of "blended" families. Such cross- cultural relationships could be comparable to what biology professor Keeney (1983) defined as "ecological climax" a "vital equilibrium" of various forms of experiencing and behavior in an environment. A challenging and complicated relationship might also be a treatment for apathy.

In India, women play a very small part in making decisions about their husbands and the traditions and rituals that would be followed during their marriages. Indian women are known to have limited independence and directing potential (Bloom, Wypij and Das Gupta, 2001, et al). According to Basu (1992), Dyson and Moore, 1983, et al., women have very limited permission within the family which is linked to numerous consequences which are high level of fertility and discernment in source provision in the family. Since ancient times, the couple's parents and the extended family have taken up the responsibility to find a partner for their son/daughter's marriage. They have a very big influence in the children's marriage, so much so that the children meet their partner when they are about to get married.

According to Rathor (2003), there is a rise in inter-caste marriages in India, specifically amongst few socio-economic group such as urban youth. Inter-culture marriage has been in the rise in India because of urbanization and development in socio-economic status. According to Singh, Goli and Sekher (2013), there has been numerous differences in socio-economic status which has been recorded among inter-culture marriages and how it is affected their arrays of marriage. A researcher Pande (2015) speaks about how few south Asian women are able to assume command while selecting their spouse for marriage even in arranged marriages.

In India, there are various important conditions which are important for choosing a partner for marriage and one of the important aspects is caste. Caste is prescribed and not ascribed. It is also a very essential part of Hinduism. As a result, it is firmly ingrained in Indian society and culture. The most common type of marriage is monogamy, and very few societal communities tolerate divorce, which increases the forces of the caste dynamic. According to Srinivasan and James, 2015, it is very important to cautiously choose a life mate. Inter-caste and inter-religious marriages are subsequently detested and looked down upon by society. A researcher Kannan (1963) has studied 149 inter-caste marriages in Bombay city. He learned that inter-caste marriage has just in recent times been constantly increasing and that it has become an important factor since 1956. Inter-caste marriages in Bombay are influenced by a number of serious aspects, including the women's age at the time of marriage, the freedom granted to her to pick her spouse, and the level of education received by women. According to a study constructed on evidence from matrimonial advertisements, the caste barricade is altering in some families and more people are inviting inter-caste marriages. The majority of the time, friends and family will recourse to dishonest ways to prevent such unions, yet this propensity has risen from 700 inter-caste weddings recorded in West Bengal in 1955 to 5800 in 1969. The highest ranking caste the Brahmins are the most hostile to inter-caste unions. Hindus, including Kayasthas, Baidyas, and others, are gradually becoming more accepting of inter-caste unions. Postgraduates are also more accepting of inter- caste marriage than undergraduates and graduates (Sarkar, 1970). There was a study which was conducted in the rural areas of Andra Pradesh in which many people preferred their sons and daughters to have got them married into their own caste, but very few people were opposed to this thought. There was another study which was done on inter-caste marriage which recorded that the parents preferred inter-caste marriages more than getting married into their own caste. He additionally sees that inter-caste marriage takes place at fairly advanced age rather than at the young age. Andra Pradesh and Maharashtra had at least around 1000 inter-caste marriages in 3 years. Despite being a very important and complicated social topic in the Indian setting, there isn't much literature on inter-caste marriage. This may be because there isn't enough information or because there are issues with it. There are intermittent ethnographic researches, which by classification cannot be comprehensive. The main aspects which contribute to inter-caste marriage are level of education, socio-economic status, urban residence, and employment. Even though there are many parents who haven't given a liking to inter-caste or inter-culture marriage, many of them have accepted the inter-caste and inter-culture marriages and have started to respect their children's choice for choosing their partner for marriage.

Culture in Minangkabau Women's Marriage

Another case is cultural values affect Minangkabau women who marry men from another culture. Both urban and rural societies, including Padang, Pariaman, Agam, Tanah Datar, 50 Kota, Payakumbuh, and Solok, are home to the ladies. The women have been married for more than five years and have a range of education qualification, from senior high school to a university. The arrangement of husband-and-wife relations in Indonesian society establishes how important the cultural component is to their communications. This cultural component has an effect on how Minangkabau women are built. In Minangkabau society, women are viewed as active, accepting of masculinity, capable of taking on tasks and cooperating with males. Some researchers have looked on the ideal position of women in Indonesia.

In the study done by researchers found that, the Minangkabau wives have the authority to run a home. Although marrying men from other ethnic groups, Minangkabau women uphold their cultural beliefs. In the study, researchers have studied about two adaptations i.e., adaptation to the couple and adaptation to the couple's family. A Minangkabau woman will try to blend in with her husband's family, who are of another race and culture, in order to preserve peace in their homes. There are three communication phases that both the families intend to get married must go through in order to reach an agreement. The tradition that will be followed for the wedding ceremony comes first. Either the groom's family tradition will be used or the bride's family tradition will be used or both the tradition will be used alternatively.

Even though the ceremony will not be complicated, 37 informants said that if the woman id from Minangkabau culture, then the ceremony will be held in her house. If the daughter is not getting married due to financial issues, then as per her culture, the bride's extended family is allowed to mortgage the customary land. In the culture if there is a daughter is still not married, it is shame for the family. The second negotiation is that the rooms which are available in the household should be occupied by the woman, the husband and their children. The woman and the parent's relationship after her marriage is still strong, if the husband is to be a part of his wife's family, then he should be on his best behavior and be respectful towards her extended family and parents. Minangkabau women don't have a very tight relationship with her husband's family. Minangkabau women have limited interaction with her husband's family during the holidays before the month of Ramadan, Eid al-Fitr, Eid al-Adha and during weddings. The Minangkabau had the power to main the household so much more than her husband, which meant that the whole responsibility of their children's care and the household maintenance fell on her shoulder. It is sense of pride for them. Women in Minangkabau culture have taken the role of being break makers and deal the economic situation in the family. It means that they have the key to taking care of assets such as rice, fields and properties.

In a study conducted, the researchers studied how women's experiences with cross-cultural transformation influenced their perception of intercultural relationships. In this research, they examined how women felt that cross culture affected their marriage, specifically with regards to values and culture and role taking, how the women were benefitted for moving across cultures for their spouse. 15 non-Chilean women were interviewed who were married to Chilean women, the women had lived with their parents and lived in their native and moved to their husband's home when they got married. They found out that, all the participants preserved at least few of their cultures despite the societal pressure after moving to their husband's house. Adding to those, 11 women appealed to have adopted Chilean ethics, such as being more laid-back about time and schedules and open with their affection, which positively affected their families. Women who reported altering gender roles in their connections either observed it as circumstantial as they instantaneously became stay-at-home mothers or as a direct result of moving to a culture that maintained firmer ideas of male-female role taking. Regardless of the fact that about half of the women said they had to give up their careers, the majority of them believed that moving to Chile had positively affected their characters as mothers, wives, and women because domestic help was more rationally valued there and the country's culture was more child-friendly. Most women talked about the challenges they had to face after moving to a new country and culture, few of them talked about how moving to a different culture had helped to strengthen their relationship. They stated that they had to have a lot patience and they had good communication between them in their marriage and they were willing to cooperate with each other were some of their best qualities in their relationship.

Some latest studies show that inter-cultural marriages have been growing in the United States, Australia, Canada and among other countries of Europe. Another research that showed that inter-cultural is a phenomenon which has been growing a lot in Europe, America, and East Asia. Some research show that in Helsinki, these kinds of marriages are more communal is currently at the rate of 12 percent, and marriages between Finnish national and a foreign national comprised of 15 percent of all marriages in Helsinki in 2011.

Cross-culture marriage has become an essential part of society and their numbers have been increasing in almost all the countries. Because of different culture, values and belief system, there might be conflicts with the family.

Family resilience is well-defined as the ability to endure, adjust, fight and be strong when dealing with crises. There are two views through which we can understand the two concepts of resilience. Firstly, resilience is an individual's personality to be able to endure in an emergency. This notion is utterly correct because resilience cannot be constructed or established if resilience is measured as a personality. Secondly, resilience is a process. It can be established and succeeded.

George Kelly a researcher supported personal construct theory which served as the groundwork for the expansion of family resilience. Numerous studies on resilience have been accompanied at the individual level and in a more multifaceted setting, particularly the household. According to the family resilience theory, a family under a lot of stress can continue to function normally despite the effects of adversity. Adding, Bradley & Hojjat's research points to the value of family resilience in nurturing married pleasure. Family resilience is determined by numerous aspects. One of them is culture. Culture is a basis of strength for families to adjust and form families, but on the other hand, culture can also be a danger.

Intercultural marriages have been increasing and there is at least over 21% of married couple have at least one foreign-born partner. All kinds of marriages have challenges, and there is conversation of differences. However, intercultural marriages involve disputes about two cultures, their norms and view of extended family, religion and beliefs. For example, couples may have a communication about which religious holidays to celebrate, parenting styles, child-rearing, they also face challenges, negative stereotype, discrimination, or rejection (Stritof, 2020). But there are positive benefits to inter-culture marriage. Couples in inter-culture relationship establish a stronger bond in their relationship and their own sense of identity.

Conclusion

Inter-cultural couples go through challenges of cultural adjustment. Marriage between people from various cultures is a discussing process since it implies the change from dual personality to partnership within a relationship. Though there are differences in the culture, cultural norms and beliefs, communication skills and patience and understanding is very important for a relationship to work, just how there are misunderstanding in a marriage, communication is the first important step for any relationship. There are still many aspects of cross-cultural marriages that haven't been researched extensively; nevertheless, what research has been done suggests that while there are differences, the couple's connection is greater than ever, and it also helps to have the support of their in-laws, friends, and family.

References

Falicov. C. J., (1995) Cross Cultural Marriages Retrived from : https://www.researchgate.net/publication/264092016_Cross_Cultural_Marriages.

A.M. Sultana. (2021) INTER-CULTURAL MARITAL RELATIONSHIP: RECRUITING PARTICIPANTS FROM BANGLADESHI COMMUNITY

Ani. A., Nadya. A., Setiowati. A. (2021). Cross-Cultural Marriage Family Resilience and Implications for Family Guidance and Counseling

Bradley, J. M., & Hojjat, M. (2016). A model of resilience and marital satisfaction. the Journal of Social Psychology/ Journal of Social Psychology, 157(5), 588–601. https://doi.org/10.1080/00224545.2016.1254592

Bloom SS, Wypij D, Das Gupta M. (2001) Dimensions of women's autonomy and the influence on maternal health care utilization in a north Indian city. Demography. 2001 Feb;38(1):67-78. doi: 10.1353/dem.2001.0001. PMID: 11227846.

Calderon. K. N (2012) The impact of cross-cultural transition on intercultural relationships using a strengths-based approach

Chhetri. C. (2019). Cross Cultural Marriages and the Problem of Adjustment in Conjugal Life.

Cheung, M. (2005). A cross-cultural comparison of gender factors contributing to long-term marital satisfaction: A narrative analysis. Journal of Couples and Relationship Therapy, 4(1), 51-78.

Crohn, J. (1986). Ethnic identity and marital conflict: Jews, Italians and WASPs, New York: AMaican Jewish Committee, Institute for Human Relations

Dewi. S. F., Montessori. M., Saputra. R. A. Farsalena. S., Fatmariza. F., et al, (2019). The Role of Culture in Cross-Cultural Marriage among Minangkabau Women

Dyson T. and Moore T. 1983. On kinship structure, female autonomy, and demographic behaviour in India. Population and Development Review, 9(1): 35-54.

Falicov, C. J. (1995). Cross cultural marriages. ResearchGate. Retrived from: https://www.researchgate.net/publication/ 264092016_Cross_Cultural_Marriages

Falicov, C. J. (1998). The cultural meaning of family triangles. In M. McGoldrick (Ed.), Re-visioning family therapy: Race, culture, and gender in clinical practice (pp. 37–49). The Guilford Press.

Falicov, C. J. (1998) Learning to Think culturally. In H. A., Liddle & D.C. Bruenlin & R.CSchwartz (Eds,),

Handbook of family therapy training and supervision. New York : Guliford Press

Frame, M. W. (2004). The challenges of intercultural marriage: Strategies for pastoral care. Pastoral. Psychology, 52, 2 1 9-232. Gaines..

Goli, S., Singh, D., & Sekher, T. V. (2013). Exploring the Myth of Mixed Marriages in India: Evidence from a Nation-wide Survey. Journal of Comparative Family Studies, 44(2), 193–206. https://doi.org/10.3138/jcfs.44.2.193.

Kannan, C.T., (1963), Inter-caste marriages in Bombay, Allied Publishers Private Limited, Bombay.

Keney, B. P. (1983). Aesthetics of change. New York: Guildford Press.

Kumar. H. A. (2021) INTER-MARRIAGES IN INDIA: A REVIEW OF LITURATURE.

Machette. A., Cionea. L., (2022) In-laws, Communication, and Other Frustrations: The Challenges of Intercultural Marriages

Pande, R. (2014). 'I arranged my own marriage': arranged marriages and post-colonial feminism. Gender, Place and Culture, 22(2), 172–187. https://doi.org/ 10.1080/0966369x.2013.855630

Schilz, D. (1976). The changing family: Its function and future. Englewood Cliffs, NJ: Prentice-Hall.

Stritof, S. (2020, January 29). Challenges of an interracial marriage from society. verywellmind. https://www.verywellmind.com/interracial-marriage-challenges-2303129

UK Essays. (November 2018). Cross Cultural Marriage Essay. Retrieved from: https://www.ukessays.com/essays/cultural-studies/inter-cultural- marriage-analysis-cultural-studies-essay.php?vref=1

Winch, R. (1995). The theory of Complementary needs in mate selection: Final results on the test of the general hypothesis. American Sociological Review, 20, 553-555

Wong, S., & Goodwin, R. (2009). The impact of work on marriage in three cultures: a qualitative study. Community, Work & Family, 12(2), 213–232. https://doi.org/10.1080/13668800902778975

CHAPTER THIRTEEN

Voices Across Cultures: How Cultural Context Shapes Communication

- Akshyata Giri

Background

Communication is a fundamental aspect of human interaction, essential for sharing ideas, feelings, and information. It is a complex process influenced by numerous factors, including cultural background. Culture shapes how individuals perceive and engage in communication, impacting everything from language use to non-verbal cues. This chapter explores the intricate relationship between culture and communication, examining how cultural differences affect both verbal and non-verbal interactions.

Communication techniques have historically changed in tandem with human societies. Social standards and cultural values had a big impact on early communication methods like pictographs and gestures. Communication systems evolved alongside cultures to become increasingly complex. Language, writing systems, and, more recently, digital communication tools have all developed in close connection with the formation of culture. We may better grasp how cultural influences have influenced the way we communicate and process information now when we are aware of the historical background of communication. Conventional evaluations of communication frequently overlook the subtle ways that culture affects communication. People from diverse cultural origins may be at a disadvantage due to the bias that certain standardised examinations and measurements have towards particular cultural norms.

The chapter aims to explore the ways in which culture shapes communication and also includes a qualitative study conducted in order to understand the same. By examining various elements such as language, social norms, and cultural values, it provides a comprehensive understanding of how culture influences both verbal and non-verbal communication. This exploration is intended to better appreciate the diversity of communication styles and the importance of cultural sensitivity.

Review of Literature

Communication is not just about exchanging words; it encompasses a wide range of verbal and non-verbal behaviors influenced by cultural contexts. Studies have consistently demonstrated that communication patterns are greatly influenced by culture. The idea of high-context and low-context cultures, introduced by Hall in 1976, is fundamental to comprehending these distinctions. High-context cultures, like those in China and Japan, mostly rely on non-verbal clues and implicit communication. Low-context cultures, like those in Germany and the United

States, on the other hand, value clear, concise communication. Understanding how cultural backgrounds influence communication choices and behaviours requires an awareness of this divide. Language serves as both a major means of communication and a crucial marker of cultural identity. Sapir-Whorf hypothesis holds that vision and mind are shaped by language. Research conducted by Bonvillain (2019) has indicated that people's worldviews are influenced by language structures. Languages that have many phrases for the same notion, such as Inuit languages, which have many terms for snow, are examples of languages that reflect interactions between the environment and cultural goals.

Cultural standards have a significant impact on nonverbal communication, which includes body language, facial expressions, and gestures. While basic emotions are understood by all people, there can be considerable cultural differences in the ways that these emotions are presented and interpreted, according to Ekman's (1972) research on facial expressions. For instance, making eye contact is a frequent non-verbal indicator that in Western cultures can indicate honesty and confidence, but in certain Asian cultures, it may be interpreted as disrespectful. Acceptable communication styles in social situations are determined by cultural standards. According to Monippally (2001), these norms have an impact on everything from greeting customs to dispute resolution techniques. Harmony and social cohesion are valued in collectivist societies, such those seen in East Asia, which results in more indirect communication techniques. Individualist cultures—such as those seen in the West—value boldness and self-expression, which leads to more straightforward communication. Cultural sensitivity is critical to ethical communication practices because it promotes understanding and respect amongst people with different backgrounds. Abdulla (2018) stresses that in order to prevent miscommunication, disputes, and even ethical transgressions, it is critical to acknowledge and honour cultural differences in communication. Understanding cultural quirks and being able to modify communications to fit the audience's cultural norms and beliefs are prerequisites for ethical communication.

Findings and Discussion

A study utilized a qualitative approach to explore how culture influences communication among 20 female undergraduate students aged 17-19, representing diverse backgrounds. The goal was to capture detailed insights into participants' communication experiences and perceptions. With a series of 20 questions addressing communicative comfort, fear of judgement, and cultural influences, semi-structured interviews were used to collect the data. The conversation topics included the participants' communication methods, encounters with cross-cultural relationships, and cultural influences. Prior consent was obtained from each participant, who were informed of their right to withdraw from the study at any stage.

Thematic analysis identified patterns in interview transcripts, highlighting themes such as comfort level, fear of judgement, anxiousness, key moments, parents' influence. Interviews were transcribed verbatim, and themes were coded based on recurring topics and insights.

Participants unanimously emphasized that their comfort level significantly influenced their communication. They expressed that feeling at ease with someone was crucial for initiating and maintaining conversations. For example, participants stated that they preferred talking to those they felt comfortable with, which facilitated open communication. Many participants acknowledged a strong fear of being judged by others based on their communication abilities. They often mentioned hesitating to interact with new people out of concern for negative perceptions. Participants shared experiences where this fear of judgement inhibited their willingness to initiate conversations. Several participants reported feeling anxious, especially when communicating with unfamiliar individuals or in public settings. They linked this anxiousness to the fear of being negatively evaluated, which made it challenging for them to communicate effectively. Participants described instances where their anxiety affected their communication behavior. The individuals mentioned particular incidents that had a big impact on their attitudes and communication abilities. These "key moments" included embarrassing public experiences or encouraging encounters that influenced their self-assurance. Participants shared stories, for instance, of events that either increased or decreased their confidence in speaking up. Participants reflected on how parental attitudes and behaviors impacted their communication abilities. Positive parental encouragement and opportunities for social interaction were seen as supportive factors that facilitated better communication skills. Conversely, participants mentioned challenges in communication when parental attitudes were restrictive or less encouraging. These recurring themes highlight the complex interplay of comfort levels, fear of judgement, anxiousness, impactful experiences, and parental influences in shaping individuals' communication behaviors and experiences.

Conclusion

Communication is profoundly influenced by culture, shaping its forms, structures, and styles. This connection significantly impacts how individuals both transmit and interpret messages, encompassing both verbal and nonverbal dimensions. The study's findings underscore the critical importance of cultural awareness in fostering effective communication, particularly within diverse and multicultural environments. Participants' reflections on their cultural backgrounds, upbringings, and life experiences highlighted how these factors intricately mold communication styles. This introspective exploration provided deeper insights into personal identity and the multifaceted influences shaping communication behaviors. The research illuminated how familial environments and cultural diversity distinctly shape individuals' approaches to communication. Ultimately, it revealed how cultural contexts contribute to the nuanced variations in communication styles observed among participants.

While this study provides valuable insights into the impact of culture on communication, it is not without limitations. The sample size was limited to 20 female undergraduate students, which may not be representative of the broader population. Additionally, the qualitative nature of the research, based on personal interviews, may introduce subjective biases. Future research should aim to include a more diverse sample and employ quantitative methods to obtain more generalizable results. This study paves way to understand subjective differences in cultural upbringing and the way it effects each individual with the way they communicate. Understanding different cultures and a person's upbringing might be able to way a lot about why they communicate the way they do. Along with various opportunities given later in life, how does the opportunities given earlier in life be able to determine the way a person is able to communicate.

References

Abdulla, M.R. (2018). Culture, religion, and freedom of religion or belief. The Review of Faith & International Affairs, 16(4), pp. 102-115.

Bâlc, S. (2018). The relationship between culture and communication within the Ecclesia. Advances in Social Science, Education and Humanities Research, 211, pp. 258-264.

Bonvillain, N. (2019). Language, culture, and communication: The meaning of messages. Rowman & Littlefield Publishers.

Brown, N., McIlwraith, T., & de González, L.T. (2020). Perspectives: An open introduction to cultural anthropology (2nd ed.). The American Anthropological Association.

Croucher, S.M. (2020). The importance of culture and communication. Frontiers in Communication, 5, p. 61.

Creanza, N., Kolodny, O., & Feldman, M. W. (2017). Cultural evolutionary theory: How culture evolves and why it matters. Proceedings of the National Academy of Sciences, 114(30), pp. 7782-7789.

Ekman, P. (1972). *Universals and cultural differences in facial expressions of emotion*. University of Nebraska Press.

Gao, B., & VanderLaan, D. P. (2020). Cultural influences on perceptions of emotions depicted in emojis. Cyberpsychology, Behavior, and Social Networking, 23(8), pp. 567-570.

Glassdoor Team. (2021). The effect of culture in communication. Glassdoor.

Graca, S. S., & Barry, J. M. (2017). Culture impact on perceptions of communication effectiveness. International Business Research, 10(1), pp. 116-128.

Hall, B.J., Covarrubias, P.O., & Kirschbaum, K.A. (2017). Among cultures: The challenge of communication (3rd ed.). Routledge.

Hall, E. T. (1976). Beyond Culture. Anchor Books.

University of Houston-Victoria. (2020). How does culture affect communication?. University of Houston-Victoria.

Hunley, B., Chakraborty, S., & MacDonald, S. (2018). The impact of cultural communication on team performance. Engineering and Technology Management Student Projects, pp. 1-12.

Kamalipour, Y.R. (2019). Global communication: A multicultural perspective. Rowman & Littlefield.

Lewens, T. (2017). Human nature, human culture: the case of cultural evolution. Interface focus, 7(5), pp. 1-7.

Mansouri, F. (2017). Interculturalism at the crossroads: Comparative perspectives on concepts, policies and practices. UNESCO Publishing.

McLeod, S. (2017). Communication rights: Fundamental human rights for all. International Journal of Speech-Language Pathology, 20(1), pp. 3-11.

Monippally, M. M. (2001). *Business communication: Strategies and skills*. Oxford University Press.

Poepsel, M. (2018). Media, society, culture and you. Rebus Community.

Stadler, S. (2019). Conflict, culture and communication (1st ed.). Routledge.

StudyCorgi. (2022, October 29). The Impact of Culture on Communication. Retrieved from https://studycorgi.com/the-impact-of-culture-on-communication/

Szkudlarek, B., Osland, J. S., Nardon, L., & Zander, L. (2020). Communication and culture in international business–Moving the field forward. Journal of World Business, 55(6), pp. 1-9.

The National Academy of Sciences. (2018). Addressing the social and cultural norms that underlie the acceptance of violence: proceedings of a workshop – in brief. The National Academies Press.

Xiaomeng, H. U., Feng, Y. U., & Kaiping, P. E. N. G. (2018). How does culture affect morality? The perspectives of between-culture variations, within-culture variations, and multiculturalism. Advances in Psychological Science, 26(11), pp. 2081-2090.

CHAPTER FOURTEEN

Bridging the Gap: Understanding Ethnocentrism Across Generations

- Anokha V

Background

A universal phenomenon that impacts social interactions is ethnocentrism. It's a vague idea that's used by different people and fields in different ways that are inconsistent and conflicting. This theory was first applied in 1906 by sociologist William Graham Sumner. There are numerous distinct manifestations of ethnocentrism, including biased or discriminating beliefs, behaviors, or laws that favor one's own group over others. It is a key idea in the disciplines of anthropology, psychology, sociology, and political science. Stereotypes and intercultural conflict arise from the perception of cross-cultural differences, which is often influenced by ethnocentrisms. It involves making conclusions about representatives of different cultures based on many factors, such as their unique dialects and manners. Ethnocentrism affects one's propensity to engage in cross-cultural interactions. In this sense, studies have found that an individual's inclination to communicate in cross-cultural contexts declines as ethnocentrism increases. It has also been found to preserve people's affection for their own culture and influence how they view other civilizations.This fosters stereotyping among the individuals. Even though it begins personally, it could affect the entire community.

The subtle aspects of ethnocentrism are discussed in this chapter, with a focus on the differences and similarities between the attitudes of young adolescents and older people, as well as the social, cognitive, and developmental factors that influence these attitudes.

Ethnocentrism is the tendency to see other groups and cultures through the lens of one's own ethnic group, along with the notion that one's own ethnic group or culture is inherently superior. Prejudice, discrimination, and hostility toward people from diverse cultural or racial backgrounds are frequently the outcomes of this concept (Sumner, 2019). It is regarded as a perverted kind of racism when people act negatively toward members of other ethnic groups in addition to favouring members of their own (Stephan & Stephan, 1996). This sense of community encourages prejudice against the outside group and in-group bias, which frequently results in ethnocentric beliefs and actions. It can take many different forms, ranging from covert prejudice and stereotyping to overt antagonism and discrimination.

The developmental phases of young adolescents and older individuals are distinct and have distinctive qualities that impact their ethnocentric attitudes. Adolescence is a crucial time for identity formation because it is during this time that people are most vulnerable to peer pressure and social pressures, which frequently reinforces in-group bias and denigration of out-group members (Erikson, 1968). Teenagers' perspectives on ethnicity and cultural variety are greatly influenced by their peer groups, families, and the media (Aboud & Doyle, 1996).

Older persons may have strongly ingrained ethnocentric sentiments due to their unique historical and social backgrounds. More ingrained ethnocentric beliefs in later life might result from a lifetime of exposure to certain cultural norms and values, cognitive rigidity, and social isolation (Pettigrew, 1998; Rokeach, 1960). Yet, elements like community involvement and lifelong learning have the power to question and even change these beliefs (Marsiske, Lang, Baltes, & Baltes, 1995).

Ethnocentrism among Adolescents

Adolescence is a developmental stage marked by black-and-white thinking, which can help create a mentality of "us vs. them" (Piaget, 2013). The formation of ethnocentric sentiments in teenagers is greatly influenced by peer groups. According to Abourd and Doyle (1996), adolescents may exhibit ethnocentric ideas and behaviors as a result of their peer's acceptance and support. Teenagers who have friends from a variety of origins are less likely to be ethnocentric than teenagers who have homogeneous friend groups, which emphasizes the importance of social exposure in lowering ethnocentric beliefs (Feddes, Noack, & Rutland, 2009).

Although this process differs among people, teenagers may start to examine and reject ethnocentric views as they advance through stages of moral reasoning (Kohlberg, 1987).Through the promotion of awareness and respect of cultural variety, multicultural education programs in schools have been demonstrated to diminish ethnocentric attitudes among teenagers (Banks, 2009). The idea that puberty inevitably results in the development of ethnocentric attitudes is challenged by the fact that adolescents exposed to various surroundings, such as multicultural neighborhoods or schools, frequently acquire more inclusive attitudes and exhibit lower levels of ethnocentrism (Phinney, Ferguson, & Tate, 1997).Adolescents' growing use of social media and international media can lessen ethnocentric views and increase cultural understanding by exposing them to a variety of viewpoints (Yim, 2003).

Ethnocentrism among Older Adults

According to Pettigrew (1998), older persons frequently have more ingrained attitudes as a result of their lifetime exposure to particular cultural norms and values, which can support ethnocentric viewpoints. The social and historical circumstances that earlier generations have encountered, such as times of strong nationalism, can greatly influence how they view ethnicity and perpetuate ethnocentric ideas (Sherif & Sherif, 1953).

According to Rokeach (1960), cognitive flexibility tends to decline with age, which makes older persons less able to adopt new viewpoints and more prone to cling to long-held ethnocentric attitudes. Due to restricted connection with other groups, social isolation in older persons might reinforce preexisting ethnocentric ideas and reduce opportunities for opposing them (Cuddy, Norton, & Fiske, 2005).

In contrast to the notion of cognitive rigidity, some elderly people exhibit flexibility in their views toward different cultures and a lifetime of learning and adaptation (Marsiske, Lang, Baltes, & Baltes, 1995). According to

Cornwell, Laumann, and Schumm (2008), older persons who continue to be involved in various societies and engage in social activities tend to display more inclusive attitudes, which challenges the notion of older adults being universally ethnocentric.

Comparison of Ethnocentrism between Adolescents and Adults

Different age groups' media consumption habits have an impact on their ethnocentric viewpoints. While older adults may prefer conventional media that may encourage ethnocentric attitudes, younger people are more likely to interact with global media and social platforms that promote diversity. Multicultural education is beneficial to younger generations since it tries to lessen ethnocentric views and encourage inclusivity. Perhaps in their educational experiences, older generations placed less of a focus on ethnic diversity. Different historical periods' social movements, political environments, and economic shifts influence how successive generations view ethnicity. Differences in ethnocentric sentiments can be attributed to cultural and societal changes that have occurred across successive generations.

Conclusion

Without a doubt, one should not undervalue the importance of ethnocentrism.It is a necessary component of human existence and might not be entirely eliminated. It was stated that despite all of the assertions to the contrary, we all seem to be ethnocentric and that we are unable to completely escape our ethnocentrism. If we wish to put an end to ethnocentrism in its most severe manifestations, it also suggests that we still have personal work to do.

Insights about ethnocentrism across a variety of age groups can be useful in creating conflict-reduction and intergroup-improvement methods. Comprehending the developmental dimensions of ethnocentrism enables the development of educational initiatives and interventions that are age-appropriate and promote inclusive perspectives. Understanding ethnocentrism is essential for improving cultural competency and intergroup communication in today's globalized society. Adolescents may not benefit from the same strategies as older adults, and vice versa. Customized strategies that take into account the distinct social, cognitive, and developmental aspects at work can produce better results in fostering social cohesion and lowering intergroup conflict.

However, Ethnocentrism would hold on to certain limitations as well. Self-reported data is frequently used, and social desirability bias has the potential to cause people to underreport their ethnocentric views. The dynamic character of ethnocentrism across time may be lost in cross-sectional research, which do not account for how views change with aging and shifting social settings. The lack of proper control over cultural and socioeconomic characteristics makes it difficult to generalize research findings across diverse groups.Also, cognitive decline —which is not frequently taken into account in studies—may have an impact on older persons' ethnocentrism. Mostly, the impact of schooling and media on the views of adolescents is intricate and diverse, necessitating further extensive and long-term studies to completely comprehend their long-term consequences.

Through addressing the unique requirements and effects of every age group, we can strive towards a world that is more understanding and tolerant. Thus, it is not necessary for us to take a neutral stance. We should be excited about the universe and never allow ourselves to treat someone disrespectfully as long as we remember that we are all a part of it.

References

Aboud, F. E., & Doyle, A. B. (1996). Parental and peer influences on children's racial attitudes. International Journal of Intercultural Relations, 20(3-4), 371-383.

Banks, J. A. (Ed.). (2009). The Routledge international companion to multicultural education (pp. 9-32). New York: Routledge.

Cornwell, B., Laumann, E. O., & Schumm, L. P. (2008). The social connectedness of older adults: A national profile. American sociological review, 73(2), 185-203.

Cuddy, A. J., Norton, M. I., & Fiske, S. T. (2005). This old stereotype: The pervasiveness and persistence of the elderly stereotype. Journal of social issues, 61(2), 267-285.

Erikson, E. H. (1968). Identity youth and crisis (No. 7). WW Norton & company.

Feddes, A. R., Noack, P., & Rutland, A. (2009). Direct and extended friendship effects on minority and majority children's interethnic attitudes: A longitudinal study. Child development, 80(2), 377-390.

Kohlberg, L. (1987). The psychology of moral development. Ethics, 97(2).

Marsiske, M., Lang, F. R., Baltes, P. B., & Baltes, M. M. (1995). Selective optimization with compensation: Life-span perspectives on successful human development. Compensating for psychological deficits and declines: Managing losses and promoting gains, 35-79.

Marsiske, M., Lang, F. R., Baltes, P. B., & Baltes, M. M. (1995). Selective optimization with compensation: Life-span perspectives on successful human development. Compensating for psychological deficits and declines: Managing losses and promoting gains, 35-79.

Pettigrew, T. F. (1998). Intergroup contact theory. Annual review of psychology, 49(1), 65-85.

Pettigrew, T. F. (1998). Intergroup contact theory. Annual review of psychology, 49(1), 65-85.

Phinney, J. S., Ferguson, D. L., & Tate, J. D. (1997). Intergroup attitudes among ethnic minority adolescents: A causal model. Child development, 68(5), 955-969.

Piaget, J. (2013). The moral judgment of the child. Routledge.

Rokeach, M. (1960). The open and closed mind: Investigations into the nature of belief systems and personality systems.

Rokeach, M. (1960). The open and closed mind: Investigations into the nature of belief systems and personality systems.

Sherif, M., & Sherif, C. W. (1953). Groups in harmony and tension; an integration of studies of intergroup relations.

Stephan, W. G., & Stephan, C. W. (1996). Predicting prejudice. International journal of intercultural relations, 20(3-4), 409-426.

Sumner, W. G. (2019). Folkways: A study of the sociological importance of usages, manners, customs, mores, and morals. Good Press.

Yim, J. (2003). Audience concentration in the media: Cross-media comparisons and the introduction of the uncertainty measure. Communication Monographs, 70(2), 114-128.

CHAPTER FIFTEEN

Cultural Pathways to Healing: Intersection of Tradition and Modern Psychology

- **Nila Nidhi**

Background

It is very important to understand how culture has an influence on the decision to seek psychological help among individuals. An individuals cultural background tends to have a huge impact on their opinions, beliefs, and attitudes toward seeking psychological help or treatment. Therefore, understanding how culture can shape their help-seeking behaviours may help provide more information on improving mental health services. The impact of culture on seeking psychological help can also strengthen efforts to improve overall mental health services and reduce any gaps among the underprivileged populations. To deliver this care that is sensitive to cultural differences, mental health practitioners must also try to comprehend and value these distinctions. There is an obvious necessity to understand the cultural impacts, but there has very few research done on how cultural backgrounds can have an affect on an individuals' propensity to seek psychological help.

Cultural factors can have an influence on how people perceive mental health and the extent to which they seek psychological help. The decision to seek help and the expectations and experiences with mental health services can all be influenced by cultural factors including beliefs ,values and traditions. Mental health disorders are sometimes seen as a moral or spiritual concern in certain cultures, while others see it as a sign of weakness. Seeking assistance from a mental health professional could be interpreted in some cultures as a reflection of mistrust toward community and family members who are typically there to offer support and direction. Furthermore, people seeking mental health assistance may encounter difficulties due to language barriers and cultural differences in communication styles.

According to Neighbours and Jackson (1984) and Peifer et al. (2000), individuals seek primary care from clergy and traditional healers. Traditional healers, especially among American Indians and Alaska Natives, frequently collaborate with official practitioners in tribal mental health programmes. African Americans generally tend to rely on pastors for mental health services, such as counselling and diagnosis (Levin, 1986). Some African Americans prefer to seek mental health services from therapist of their own race or ethnicity. Ethnic-specific programmes have also been developed to match clients with their therapists who share their same cultural or ethnic background (Sue, 1998). It was also noted that African Americans often tend to prefer counselling when compared to medication or drug therapy (Dwight-Johnson et al., 2000).

Each society tends to have their own sets of social and cultural norms. A set of learned behaviours and attitudes that are distinctive to a particular social group is what is meant by the term "culture," which is intergenerational. It influences the style of life and the worldview of the people who live there because of shared experiences. A few examples of these factors that can shape culture are ethnicity, race, religion, and family values. Patient's description or presentation of their symptoms to their clinicians or doctors indicates that culture has an influence on their mental health conditions. Asians are more likely to report their physical or somatic symptoms when compared to their emotional symptoms but when questioned further, they might admit to experiencing emotional symptoms (Lin & Cheung, 1997). According to Kleinman (1977,1998) patients from different cultures often selectively exhibit their symptoms in ways that they think are acceptable to them.

The suicide rates of different countries and their ethnic subgroups tend to vary drastically (Moscicki, 1995). According to studies, American Indians and Alaska Natives have the highest rates of male suicides in the United States and African American women has the lowest rates (Kachur et al., 1995). Although the main cause of the large variance in rate is still unclear , the differences in social and cultural contexts of each subgroup are likely to have an impact (van Heeringen et al., 2000; Ji et al., 2001).East Asian culture places a strong emphasize on collectivistic cultures such as social harmony and interdependence, with individuals seen as integral to a wider social unit (Markus and Kitayama, 1991). Individualistic communities, like the United States, prioritise autonomy and personal incentives over social goals (Kwan et al., 1997). Cultural values and attitudes can have an impact on help-seeking propensity (HSP) in two ways, as with any socio-cultural learning. There are two types of cultural adaptation: enculturation, which involves keeping cultural norms from one's heritage culture, and acculturation, which involves adapting to majority culture while retaining heritage norms. According to Kim (2007), Asian Americans may have a passive attitude towards seeking help due to enculturation or non-identification with mainstream American cultural values that promote it. Taylor et al. (2007), stated that Asians and Asian Americans benefit more from using implicit social support rather than seeking explicit support. European Americans gained more from explicit social support compared to implicit assistance. Kim et al. (2008), found that effective social support among Asians and Asian Americans may be linked to spending time with people rather than discussing the stressor directly.

Indian Culture

Ancient culture exhibits four distinct cultural streams which includes Indian, Egyptian, Roman and Chinese culture. The impact of supernatural forces on the human mind is a common observation in mental health issues. In several cultures, illness is viewed as an imbalance of humours that causes mental and physical distress. The Indian personality traits (sat, raj and tam) as well as the three humours (vat, pitt and kaph) , align with Chinese and Roman cultural conceptions(Gautam , 2010). . A study done by Kulhara and Chakrabarti's (2001) on "Culture and Schizophrenia and Other Psychotic Disorders" found that while schizophrenia appears to be similar globally, there are significant cultural variances. Schizophrenia outcomes appear to be better in emerging cultures than to developed ones. While the reasons for it are still unclear it is likely to influenced by culturally determined factors.

Indian Society is "collectivistic" emphasizing more on interdependence and collaboration whereas most western countries prioritise individualism. Indian and Asian families are more involved in taking care of their family members when compared to western families. Except for a few centres in South India, structured family therapy is not widely practised in India. Culture has an influence on the family structure, size and functioning by establishing certain boundaries, rules for interaction and communication patterns between them (McGill,1983). In 1982, Varma identified limitations to Western psychotherapy in India due to interdependence among Indian patients and family members and it was seen as one of the seven main challenges to dynamic and individual oriented therapy. A study done by Neki(1992) stated that privacy and confidentiality did not even exist in Indian society as privacy might isolate people in an interdependent society, therefore for treatment it was advised to try out dyadic or family therapy.

Gender Differences

People worldwide, regardless of their age or culture are affected by some sort of mental health disorders. According to the statistics, 25% of Americans who are above the age of 18 years are diagnosed to have mental health illness in a given year. As the primary cause of disability in the US, mental illnesses are linked to substance misuse, suicide and comorbid relationships. Men have the highest incidence of suicide rate when compared to women, according to the National Institute of Mental Health (NIMH,2013).

Gender role conflicted men control their emotions to prevent coming across as feminine. According to Kielski and Blazina (2009) , men find it more challenging to express their intense feelings and emotions during therapy. Men with dominant gender roles tend to self- stigmatize their view resulting in less positive attitude toward seeking psychological help (Vogel et al., 2011). Williams and Justice (2012) discovered that negative stigmas, fear and shame were the main reasons why African American students tries to avoid seeking psychological help. When it comes to help-seeking attitudes, masculine cultures like the US and Japan exhibit more gender differences than feminine cultures like Sweden and France (Nam et al., 2010).

Men are obliged to repress their emotions and solve their own problems, which might lead to a greater risk of psychological disorders(Cochran & Rabinowitz, 2000). Height and athletic abilities are the two physical stereotypes that are linked to the masculinity of men from different racial backgrounds. Asian Americans and White American men's perceptions of masculinity differ significantly, according to the research done by Wong, Horn and Chen (2013).

Various evidence has also revealed that men are considerably more reluctant compared to women when it comes to seeking professional psychological help (Cusack, Deane, Wilson, & Ciarrochi, (2006); Good & Wood, (1995); Hammer & Vogel, (2010); Johnson, Oliffe, Kelly, Galdas, & Ogrodniczuk, (2012).Few of the factors that contribute to men's unwillingness to seeking psychological help include traditional hegemonic masculine traits of being strong, tough, or even repressing feelings and emotions. (Yousaf, O., Popat, A., & Hunter, M. S. (2015),Addis & Mahalik,(2003); McCusker & Galupo,

(2011); Noone & Stephens, (2008); O'Brien, Hunt, & Hart, (2005).Most men tend to experience gender role conflict which refers to the intellectual conflicts that arise when an individual wants to defy these norms such as seeking help. Research indicates that this conflict is linked to low levels of help-seeking, presumably because men who are experiencing gender role conflict typically adhere to traditional male norms (Yousaf, O., Popat, A., & Hunter, M. S. (2015), Blazina & Watkins, (1996); Good, Dell, & Mintz, 1989; Good & Wood, (1995).

According to research, men with higher levels of education represented lower scores of conformities to masculine norms (Reilly, Rochlen, & Awad, 2013). Compared to previous masculine characteristics, Swedish modern masculinity is perceived to be more emotional, less violent and focuses on gender equality (Hearn et al., 2012). African American men usually tend to show have negative attitudes towards seeking psychological help due to their encounters with racism and cultural mistrust (Hammond, 2012). According to a researcher Vogel et al. (2011), African American men communicate expressively compared to other men and they might also feel more comfortable sharing about their personal information with a counsellor. Language competency was found to be a strong predictor for help-seeking behaviour among Asian Americans (Chu, Hsieh, and Tokars ,2011). Compared to Asian Americans, Latinos help-seeking behaviour was not correlated with their immigration age or language proficiency (Chu et al., 2011) A racial stereotype of Latino men is that they are hypersexualized , violent and inclined to mistreat women , the term "machismo" is used to characterise certain prejudices about Latino men (Arciniega, Anderson, Tovar-Blank, & Tracey, 2008).

Arciniega et al. (2008) stated that positive attributes like honour, respect and dignity were also part of a Latino men's masculine roles, therefore conventional machismo and positive attributes known as caballerismo are both integral parts of Latino masculine identity. When seeking psychological help for alcohol use disorders, Native Americans faced obstacles such as poor quality of care (Venner et al., 2012). According to research, some Native Americans find self-help group settings without other Native Americans unpleasant (Venner et al., 2012), and others fear bias and discrimination (Duran et al., 2005). It appears that Native Americans avoidance of counselling is largely due to their fear of prejudice.

Stigma

People with mental health issues may internalise stigmatising attitudes from society and feel so embarrassed of themselves as a result they tend to hide their symptoms and put off seeking psychological help (Sussman et al., 1987; Wahl, 1999). This can also limit peoples access to opportunities leading to low self-esteem, increased feelings of loneliness and hopelessness (Penn & Martin, 1998; Corrigan & Penn, 1999). The stigma surrounding mental illness is so strong in some Asian cultures that it is believed to reflect adversely on their family lineage, which affects chances for marriage and economic advancement for other family members as well (Sue & Morishima, 1982; Ng, 1997).

A cross-cultural study done on Asian Americans residing in Los Angeles focused on those who experienced symptoms and the results showed that compared to 25% of Whites, just 12 % of Asians would discuss about their mental health problems with their friends or family members. Compared to 26 % of Whites, only 4 % of Asians would see a psychiatrist or a psychologist. Additionally, compared to 13% of Whites, just 3% of Asians would visit a doctor for assistance. The study concluded that the Asian Americans in Los Angeles faced widespread and overt stigma related seeking psychological help (Zhang et al., 1998).

A national representative study discovered that view towards individuals with mental illness and ethnicity differed among people. Individuals with mental illness were viewed as more dangerous by Asian and Hispanic Americans when compared to Whites. For White people interacting with those suffering from mental illnesses lessened stigma, however this was not the case for African Americans (Whaley, 1997).

The study done by Yousaf, Popat, and Hunter (2015) on "An investigation of masculinity attitudes, gender, and attitudes toward psychological help-seeking" states how men's views towards getting psychological help relate to conventional standards of masculinity. It was also confirmed that men's reluctance to seek psychological help is greatly influenced by the societal expectations of masculinity norms account for 50% of the variability in men's help – seeking attitude. It was also notes that younger men tend to have more negative attitude towards seeking psychological help when compared to older men , potentially due to lesser experience with mental health related issues.

An article on , "Cultural Differences in Professional Help Seeking: A Comparison of Japan and the U.S." written by Mojaverian, Hashimoto, and Kim (2013) explores the cultural differences between Japanese and American students when it comes to seeking professional help. They used the Inventory of Attitudes Towards Seeking Mental

Health Services (IASMHS) to assess their help- seeking tendency, psychological openness and to understand the stigma among students in Japan and United States. The authors stated that these differences were caused by culturally specific interpersonal relationship patterns. According to the findings, Japanese students were less likely to seek professional help when compared to American students. This apprehension is partly mitigated by their inclination to seek support from close people, implying that cultural norm around informal support impact professional help-seeking behaviours.

The article on "Indian family systems, collectivistic society, and psychotherapy" written by Rakesh and Koushisk (2013) looked into the critical role of traditional joint families in mental health care. In India, family tends to play an important role when it comes to mental health, even though India is moving towards forming nuclear families. According to the authors, Family therapy may offer an efficient mental health treatment as it focuses on the advantages of Indian families and also addresses the deficit of mental health professionals in India.

Sylvia Lindinger-Sternart (2014)wrote an article on " Help-Seeking Behaviours of Men for Mental Health and the Impact of Diverse Cultural Backgrounds," which examined the reason behind men's reluctance to seek psychological help. It was stated that men are less likely to seek treatment or help when it comes to mental health problems and this resistance tends to have detrimental effects on the people and their family members. Lindinger-Sternat also stated that men's help seeking behaviours are influenced by their cultural origins. For example , few cultures strongly emphasize on preserving family honour and to avoid shame , which further inhibits men from seeking psychological help.

Conclusion

Culture tends to have a very strong influence on attitudes of individuals towards mental health issues. The history of mental health disorders, stigma and cultural norms can all influence an individual's willingness to seek professional help for mental health issues.Based on variables including location, socioeconomic class, religion, ethnicity, cultural views and beliefs regarding mental health can differ significantly. Therefore, generalising research across various cultural subgroups can be difficult. Social factors such as stigma can have a huge impact an individual's openness to disclose their mental health issues, and people may not accurately record their services. Cultural influences tend to play a multifaceted role in influencing help-seeking behaviours. Individual and systemic variables, in addition to cultural influences, can significantly affect an individual's attitudes towards mental health and their need to seek psychological help.

Improved access to appropriate mental health care for people from various cultural backgrounds requires an understanding of how culture influences help-seeking behaviour. Culturally sensitive interventions should be designed to help people and mental health professionals should also be trained to identify and overcome cultural barriers to communication. Since the impact of cultural aspects vary within the cultures, it is very critical to remember that they are not the only factors influencing on how individuals seek psychological help. Therefore, to improve mental health equity and access to everyone efforts must be taken on a comprehensive approach that considers the greater context of a individuals life experiences and beliefs. Research done on the impact of culture on seeking psychological help emphasises on the importance of culturally responsive interventions that can address the complex interaction of cultural and systemic elements that tend to influence help-seeking behaviours among people. By promoting mental health equity and enhancing access to care for individuals from varied cultural backgrounds, we may strive towards a equitable mental health system.

References

Addis, M. E., & Mahalik, J. R. (2003). Men, masculinity, and the context of help seeking. American Psychologist, 58, 5-14

Arciniega, G. M., Anderson, T. C., Tovar-Blank, Z., & Tracey, T. J. G. (2008). Toward a fuller conception of machismo: Development of a traditional machismo and caballerismo scale. Journal of Counseling Psychology, 55, 19-33. http://dx.doi.org/10.1037/0022-0167.55.1.19

Blazina, C., & Watkins, C. (1996). Masculine gender role conflict: Effects on college men's psychological well-being, chemical substance usage, and attitudes towards help seeking. Journal of Counseling Psychology, 43, 461-465

Chadda, R. K., & Deb, K. S. (2013). Indian family systems, collectivistic society and psychotherapy. Indian journal of psychiatry, 55(Suppl 2), S299-S309.

Chu, J. P., Hsieh, K-Y., & Tokars, D. A. (2011). Help-seeking tendencies in Asian Americans with suicidal ideation and attempts. Asian American Journal of Psychology, 2, 26-38. http://dx.doi.org/10.1037/a0023326.

Corrigan, P. W., & Penn, D. L. (1998). Lessons from social psychology on discrediting psychiatric stigma. American Psychologist, 54, 765–776.

Cochrank, S. V., & Rabinowitz, F. E. (2000). Men and depression: Clinical and empirical perspectives: Practical resources for the mental health professional. San Diego, CA: Academic Press.

Cusack, J., Deane, F. P., Wilson, C. J., & Ciarrochi, J. (2006). Emotional expression, perceptions of therapy, and help-seeking intentions in men attending therapy services. Psychology of Men & Masculinity, 7, 69-82

Duran, B., Oetzel, J., Lucero, J., Jiang, Y., Novins, D. K., Manson, S., & Beals, J. (2005). Obstacles for rural American Indians seeking alcohol, drug, or mental health treatment. Journal of Consulting and Clinical Psychology, 73,819-829. http://dx.doi.org/10.1037/0022-006X.73.5.819

Dwight-Johnson, M., Sherbourne, C. D., Liao, D., & Wells, K. B. (2000). Treatment preferences among primary care patients. Journal of General Internal Medicine, 15, 527–534.

Gautam, S., & Jain, N. (2010). Indian culture and psychiatry. Indian journal of psychiatry, 52(Suppl1), S309-S313.

General, U. S. (2001). Mental health: Culture, race, and ethnicity. A supplement to mental health: A report of the Surgeon General. Rockville, MD: US Department of Health and Human Services

Good, G. E., Dell, D. M., & Mintz, L. B. (1989). Male role and gender role conflict: Relations to help seeking in men. Journal of Counseling Psychology, 36, 295-300.

Good, G. E., & Wood, P. K. (1995). Male gender role conflict, depression, and help seeking: Do college men face double jeopardy? Journal of Counseling and Development, 74, 70-75

Hammer, J. H., & Vogel, D. L. (2010). Men's help seeking for depression: The efficacy of a male-sensitive brochure about counseling. The Counseling Psychologist, 38, 296-313

Hearn, J., Nordberg, M., Andersson, K., Balkmar, D., Gottzén, L., Klinth, R., . . . Sandberg, L. (2012). Hegemonic masculinity and beyond: 40 years of research in Sweden. Men and Masculinities, 1, 31-55. http://dx.doi.org/10.1177/1097184X11432113

Hammond, W. P. (2012). Taking it like a man: Masculine role norms as moderators of the racial discrimination-depressive symptoms association among African American men. American Journal of Public Health, 102, S232-S241. http://dx.doi.org/10.2105/AJPH.2011.300485

Ji, J., Kleinman, A., & Becker, A. E. (2001). Suicide in contemporary China: A review of China's distinctive suicide demographics in their sociocultural context. Harvard Review of Psychiatry, 9, 1–12

Johnson, J. L., Oliffe, J. L., Kelly, M. T., Galdas, P., & Ogrodniczuk, J. S. (2012). Men's discourses of help-seeking in the context of men's depression. Sociology of Health & Illness, 34, 345-361

Kim, B. S. K. (2007). Adherence to Asian and European American cultural values and attitudes toward seeking professional psychological help among Asian American college students. J. Couns. Psychol. 54,474–480

Kim, H. S., Sherman, D. K., and Taylor, S. E. (2008). Culture and social support. Am. Psychol. 63, 518–526

Kierski, W., & Blazina, C. (2009). The male fear of the feminine and its effects on counseling and sychotherapy Journal of Men's Studies, 17, 155-172.

Kleinman, A. (1977). Depression, somatization and the "new cross-cultural psychiatry." Social Science and Medicine, 11, 3–10.

Kleinman, A. (1988). Rethinking psychiatry: From cultural category to personal experience. New York: Free Press

Kulhara P, Chakrabarti S. Culture and schizophrenia and other psychotic disorders. Psychiatr Clin North Am 2001; 24:449-64

Kwan, V. S. Y., Bond, M. H., and Singelis, T. M. (1997). Pancultural explanations for life satisfaction: adding relationship harmony to self-esteem. J. Pers. Soc. Psychol. 73,1038–1051

Levin, J. (1986). Roles for the black pastor in preventive medicine. Pastoral Psychology, 35, 94–103

Lin, K. M., Cheung, F., Smith, M., & Poland, R. E. (1997). The use of psychotropic medications in working with Asian patients. In E. Lee (Ed.), Working with Asian Americans: A guide for clinicians (pp. 388–399). New York: Guilford Press

Markus, H. R., and Kitayama, S. (1991).Culture and the self: implications for cognition, emotion, and motivation. Psychol. Rev. 98, 224–253

McCusker, M. G., & Galupo, M. P. (2011). The impact of men seeking help for depression on perceptions of masculine and feminine characteristics. Psychology of Men & Masculinity, 12, 275-284

Moscicki, E. K. (1995). Epidemiology of suicide. International Psychogeriatrics, 7, 137–148

Mojaverian, T., Hashimoto, T., & Kim, H. S. (2013). Cultural differences in professional help seeking: A comparison of Japan and the US. Frontiers in psychology, 3, 615.

McGill D. Cultural concepts for family therapy. In: Hansen J, Falicov C, editors. Cultural Perspectives in Family Therapy: The Family Therapy Collections.

Rockville, MD: Aspen; 1983. p. 108-21

Nam, S. K., Chu, H. J., Lee, M. K., Lee, J. H., Kim, N., & Lee, S. M. (2010). A meta-analysis of gender differences in attitudes toward seeking professional psychological help. Journal of American College Health, 59, 110-116.

Neighbors, H. W., & Jackson, J. S. (1984). The use of informal and formal help: Four patterns of illness behavior in the black community. American Journal of Community Psychology, 12, 629–644

Neki JS. Confidentiality, secrecy, and privacy in psychotherapy: Sociodynamic considerations. Indian J Psychiatry 1992;34:171-3

Ng, C. H. (1997). The stigma of mental illness in Asian cultures. Australian and New Zealand Journal of Psychiatry, 31, 382–390.

NIMH National Institute of Mental Health. (2013). Transforming the understanding and treatment of mental illness through research. http://www.nimh.nih.gov/health/publications/the-numbers-count-mental-disorders-in-america/index.shtml

O'Brien, R., Hunt, K., & Hart, G. (2005). It's caveman stuff, but that is to a certain extent how guys still operate: Men's accounts of masculinity and help seeking. Social Science & Medicine, 61, 503-516.

Peifer, K. L., Hu, T. W., & Vega, W. (2000). Help seeking by persons of Mexican origin with functional impairments. Psychiatric Services, 51, 1293–1298.

Penn, D. L., & Martin, J. (1998). The stigma of severe mental illness: Some potential solutions for a recalcitrant problem. Psychiatric Quarterly, 69, 235–247.

Reilly, E. D., Rochlen, A. B., & Awad, G. H. (2013). Men's self-compassion and self-esteem: The moderating roles of shame and masculine norm adherence. Psychology of Men & Masculinity, No Pagination Specified. http://dx.doi.org/10.1037/a0031028

Sue, S. (1998). In search of cultural competence in psychotherapy and counselling. American Psychologist, 53, 440–448.

Sue, S., & Morishima, J. K. (1982). The mental health of Asian Americans. San Francisco: Jossey-Bass.

Sussman, L. K., Robins, L. N., & Earls, F. (1987). Treatment seeking for depression by black and white Americans. Social Science and Medicine, 24, 187–196.

Taylor, S. E., Welch, W. T., Kim, H. Sanad Sherman, D. K. (2007). Cultural differences in the impact of social support on psychological and biological stress responses. Psychol. Sci.18, 831–837

Yousaf, O., Popat, A., & Hunter, M. S. (2015). An investigation of masculinity attitudes, gender, and attitudes toward psychological help-seeking. Psychology of Men & Masculinity, 16(2), 234.

van Heeringen, K., Hawton, K., & Williams, J. M. G. (2000). Pathways to suicide: An integrative approach. In K. Hawton & K. van Heeringen (Eds.), The international handbook of suicide and attempted suicide (pp. 223–234). NewYork: Wiley

Varma VK. Present state of psychotherapy in India. Indian J Psychiatry 1982; 24:209-26

Venner, K. L., Greenfield, B. L., Vicuña, B., Muñoz, R., Bhatt, S., & O'Keefe, V. (2012). "I'm not one of them": Barriers to help-seeking among American Indians with alcohol dependence. Cultural Diversity and Ethnic Minority Psychology, 18, 352-362. http://dx.doi.org/10.1037/a0029757

Vogel, D. L., Heimerdinger-Edwards, S., Hammer, J. H., & Hubbard, A. (2011). "Boys don't cry". Journal of Counseling Psychology, 58, 368-382. http://dx.doi.org/10.1037/a0023688

Wahl, O. F. (1999). Mental health consumers' experience of stigma. Schizophrenia Bulletin, 25, 467–478

Williams, A., & Justice, M. (2010). Attitudes of African American males regarding counseling in four Texas universities. Education, 131, 158-168

Whaley, A. L. (1997). Ethnic and racial differences in perceptions of dangerousness of persons with mental illness. Psychiatric Services, 48, 1328–1330.

Wong, Y. J., Horn, A., & Chen, S. (2013). Perceived masculinity: The potential influence of race, racial essentialist beliefs, and stereoypes. Psychology of Men & Masculinity, 1, 1-13. http://dx.doi.org/10.1037/z0030100.

Zhang, A. Y., Snowden, L. R., & Sue, S. (1998). Differences between Asian- and White-Americans' help-seeking and utilization patterns in the Los Angeles area. Journal of Community Psychology, 26, 317–326

CHAPTER SIXTEEN

Navigating Diversity: Multicultural Awareness Across Ages and Genders

- Apshara K

Background

APA defines 'culture' as "the values, beliefs, language, rituals, traditions, and other behaviors that are passed from one generation to another within any social group. Multiculturism refers to the quality or condition of a society in which different ethnic and cultural groups have equal status and access to power but each maintains its own identity, characteristics, and mores (APA, Nd). Multicultural awareness is one the important component for a person to act appropriately in a heterogeneous society. Multicultural awareness is a process by which people understand various shared cultural beliefs, behaviors, perspectives, traditions, and values. Multicultural awareness acts as a building block to bring about inclusiveness, foster inclusive practices which in turn promote communication and collaboration among diverse people. Not only that, it reduces the stereotypes and prejudice a person would have about a person from a different culture and also promotes a sense of understanding that every culture is unique of their own and there should be no discrimination regarding that. It also makes professional settings such as a counselling session or an organization, culturally compactible for the working people from various cultural backgrounds. According to Price's Atlas of Ethnographic Societies, there are 3814 diverse cultures recorded (Foley, R. A., & Lahr, M. M, 2011). It is observable that the numbers are underestimated. Therefore, in order to be inclusive, it is hence understood that there is a necessity for multicultural awareness among people. Individuals and groups may manage the intricacies of other societies and create bonds of empathy and collaboration with the aid of multicultural awareness, which includes knowledge of religious beliefs and practices.

The chapter also articulates about culture, evolution of multiculturalism and its importance, multicultural education, multicultural awareness and its variations due to age and gender. Understanding the evolution of multiculturalism provides insights into how different cultures interact and shape social integration. It is crucial to note that multicultural and multiculturalism are not the same but goes hand in hand. According to Parekh (2000), Multicultural (per say multicultural society or environment) refers to prevalence of diversity whereas multiculturalism refers to "normative response" to that society (Safdar et al., 2023). It says that any heterogeneous society is said to be multicultural; multicultural society does not mean people have multicultural awareness or follow multiculturalism.

According to APA, Culture is "the values, beliefs, language, rituals, traditions, and other behaviors that are passed from one generation to another within any social group. Broad definitions include any socially definable group with its own set of values, behaviors, and beliefs. Accordingly, cultural groups could include groups based on shared identities such as ethnicity (e.g., German American, Blackfoot, Algerian American), gender (e.g., women, men, transgender, gender-nonconforming), sexual orientation (e.g., gay, lesbian, bisexual), and socioeconomic class (e.g., poor, working class, middle class, wealthy)." According to Hofstede (Na, 2019), culture is an innate information, that is mentally programmed element which shapes an individual's mindset, behaviors and lifestyle. It is the characteristic attitudes and behaviors of a particular group within society, such as a profession, social class, or age group. Due to different expectations and an ethnocentric attitude, there may be cultural misunderstandings, resistance, rejection, separation, problems, worry, and uncertainty.

The question which arises when reading about culture is, 'Why do we emphasise on knowing about culture when addressing multiculturalism?' The answer, one might think is 'as the word 'multiculturalism' in itself has culture in it, hence to know about culture'. Since the basic thought is correct, culture act as a base for multiculturalism which can be observed in the definitions given for multiculturalism. One such definition is given by Schalk-Soekar, Van de Vijver, & Hoogsteder (2004) define multiculturalism as "an ideology refers to the acceptance of different cultures in a society and also to the active support of these culture differences by both the majority members and minority group members" (Schalk-Soekar et al., 2004). Therefore, culture is discussed in relation to multiculturalism as it is important to recognise, value, and promote social variety. It also highlights how cultural identities are interrelated and how they support mutual comprehension, innovation, and communal cohesiveness.

Evolution of Multiculturalism

Multiculturism is the quality or condition of a society in which different ethnic and cultural groups have equal status and access to power but each maintains its own identity, characteristics, and mores. It is the promotion or celebration of cultural diversity within a society, also called cultural pluralism. Knowing the evolution of multiculturalism aids in promoting tolerance, harmony, and peaceful coexistence in diverse communities. It also helps in appreciating the diversity and complexity of societies.

Multiculturalism mainly emerged in countries where there is a significant amount of cultural diversity as well as practices and policies are created to address diversity. This pattern of immigration is mainly seen in immigrant-heavy countries like Canada, Australia, Europe, United States and United Kingdom where many ethnic groups live with one another side. Monoculturalism and assimilation prevailed before the emergence of multiculturalism Monoculturalism emphasizes normative cultural unity and homogeneity within a society. Assimilation involves merging different cultures to create a new unified culture by reducing differences. Both monoculturalism and assimilation were prevalent in nation-states since the early 19th century before the emergence of multiculturalism (Libretexts, 2024, April 3). The concept of multiculturalism has evolved differently in Western and Eastern countries.

In Western nations, multiculturalism began to take shape in the early 21st century, with many liberal democracies adopting official policies to embrace diversity. Countries like Britain and France have seen shifts in their multicultural policies over time. On the other hand, Eastern countries have also experienced the impact of multiculturalism, influenced by factors such as globalization and increased migration. The evolution of multiculturalism in these regions reflects a growing recognition of the importance of cultural diversity and the need for social integration (Sipuan, 2022). For instance, multiculturalism in the United States has evolved over time, influenced by historical events such as the civil rights movement of the 1960s. This movement led to increased cultural support for equality and tolerance, shaping the nation's ideals. Immigration laws and discrimination in the past have impacted policing practices, but norms against discrimination have gradually permeated the culture, leading to more inclusive policies (Libretexts, 2024, April 3).

The multicultural culture of Australia has evolved through time, beginning with the indigenous Aboriginal population and early British immigration. The European immigrant population that was not British added to the society's diversity. Non-European immigrants arrived after World War II, adding extra elements to the multicultural fabric. Assimilation plans were abandoned in favour of multiculturalism throughout the 1970s, which eventually resulted in the formalisation of multicultural policies in the 1980s. The acknowledgement of ethnic rights, diversity, and social cohesiveness have all benefited from this progression within Australian culture. The development of multiculturalism in Australia has been significantly influenced by Indian immigrants. They have demonstrated high income and educational levels, which puts them in a good position to adapt to the surroundings. Rapid growth in the Indian immigrant population has changed Australia's ethnic and cultural diversity. Their presence emphasises the continuous growth of diversity in Australia and helps to the country's diversified cultural environment (Na, n.d).

Importance of Multiculturalism

There are several advantages to multiculturalism for society. It encourages awareness and tolerance for diversity by understanding other cultures, languages, and customs on an equal basis. It also supports cultural heritage preservation, fostering an inclusive atmosphere that lessens social divide and fosters social cohesion. Additionally, multiculturalism fosters greater tolerance and comprehension among people while promoting creativity via the sharing of varied ideas that result in creative solutions. Additionally, it stimulates economic growth by drawing in foreign investment and generating new commercial possibilities. All things considered, multiculturalism is essential to human development since it increases empathy and improves people's perspective on the world while recognising the connections between different cultures and their pasts (Arts & Culture Council of Strathcona County, n.d.).

Another reason why multiculturalism is needed is because of intercultural conflict. Intercultural conflict is a conflict which arises when the cultural group affects the behaviour either consciously or unconsciously. It is important for people to be aware of various culture to avoid the ethnocentrism. It is also important to note that no society is culturally homogeneous. Here society refers to the people and culture refers to interactions among them.

Moreover, no two cultures are either completely similar or completely different. There can be variations and dissimilarities within the same cultural cluster. As a human develops there is a high chance of misunderstanding or disagreement which may result in conflicts. Anxiety and confusion in cross-cultural interactions are often caused by a lack of cultural awareness and interest (Gudykunst & Nishida, 2001).

A competent person or person with enough intercultural awareness abilities displays comfort and curiosity in other people's ways of life, changes viewpoints and is aware of many cultural frames of reference. Some attributes of sensitivity to the cultural differences are necessary for intercultural awareness. As an example of ethnocentrism, in India, it is not legally appropriate to have more than one partner whereas in foreign countries, there is no such restrictions. As an Indian, it is not accepted to have more than one partner and they think it is a sin to do. But it does not mean that those foreign countries' culture is wrong according to multiculturalism. Navigating conflicts between various cultural norms, addressing differences among ethnic and religious communities, and promoting tolerance are some of the challenges of multicultural awareness (Hanberger, A, 2010).

Multicultural Education and Multicultural Psychology

Multicultural education is a "progressive approach to education that emphasizes social justice, equality in education, and understanding and awareness of the traditions and language of other cultures and nationalities" (APA Dictionary of Psychology, n.d.-e). Recognizing and appreciating the distinctions between people and groups from various cultural origins is a component of multicultural awareness. Understanding and comprehending how religion influences cultural identity and worldviews is part of this. People can better appreciate the diversity and depth of human civilization by having an awareness of the various religious practises and beliefs. Individuals and groups may manage the intricacies of other societies and create bonds of empathy and collaboration with the aid of multicultural awareness, which includes knowledge of religious beliefs and practices (Kendra Cherry, 2022, April 6).

Multicultural psychology, according to APA is defined as, "an extension of general psychology that recognizes that multiple aspects of identity influence a person's worldview, including race, ethnicity, language, sexual orientation, gender, age, disability, class status, education, religious or spiritual orientation, and other cultural dimensions, and that both universal and culture-specific phenomena should be taken into consideration when psychologists are helping clients, training students, advocating for social change and justice, and conducting research" (APA Dictionary of Psychology, n.d.-f). The persistence of stereotypes and prejudice, as well as improper diagnosis and treatment, are all major effects of cultural bias in psychology.

Multicultural Awareness and Gender

Understanding gender differences and cultural diversity are essential components of building a more inclusive society. According to research done by Gudykunst & Kim (2003) on the topic "Communicating With Strangers an Approach to Intercultural Communication" found that being multiculturally aware helps promote more effective intercultural dialogue and understanding. Those who are conscious of cultural differences, for instance, are more likely to be able to negotiate difficulties in cross-cultural communication, such as variations in communication styles or social conventions. According to a study done by De Francisco (1992) on the topic "Deborah Tannen, You just don't understand: Women and men in conversation" found that there are substantial discrepancies between how men and women interact and communicate when it comes to gender. For instance, women are more likely to use language to form and maintain relationships than men, who may use it to construct hierarchy and exert dominance. Gender disparities in multicultural awareness may exist.

For instance, a study by Phinney, J. S., & Chavira, V. (1995) on the topic, "Parental ethnic socialization and adolescent coping with problems related to ethnicity" indicated that women often scored higher than men on tests of multicultural awareness. This might be because women are frequently socialised to be more perceptive of others' needs and viewpoints and more receptive to different experiences. Overall, there is evidence to show that women tend to be more multiculturally aware and competent than men, even though there may be considerable fluctuation in the findings across studies. On the other side, according to a study done by Yusri, F., & Afrida, Y (2022) on the topic, "The differences of cultural awareness based on gender, age, race, and region of the students" found that gender-based differences are not statistically significant in multicultural awareness. People share similar levels of multicultural awareness because of their age, developmental stage, and cultural knowledge gained from education. Local culture has been preserved through cultural socialization through educational content from that region. Cultural awareness can be enhanced by education and culturally-related activities, particularly those who live in multicultural environments. This similarity tries to promote understanding and social integration between people from various origins.

According to a study done by Ponce, A (2017) on the topic, "Gender and Anti-immigrant Attitudes in Europe" found that, with respect to anti-Muslim attitudes, a significant gender impact is shown, with women being more likely to have negative opinions. This suggests a change in gender dynamics brought about by the growing importance of gender equality and the stereotyping of Muslims as being gender retrograde. Though there is no strong evidence as such to prove that gender play a vital role in affecting multicultural awareness, some studies mentioned the attitude people have towards immigrants emphasis on the lack of multicultural awareness.

Multicultural Awareness across Age Groups

Multicultural awareness helps us to interact with other people from various cultural backgrounds appropriately. As there are many differences in many aspects of life due to aging. According to the study done by D'Andrea, M. (1995) on the topic "Using computer technology to promote multicultural awareness among elementary school-age students" shows that the elementary students enjoyed comparing their lifestyle with other cultured students.

According to a study done by Yusri, F., & Afrida, Y (2022) on the topic, "The differences of cultural awareness based on gender, age, race, and region of the students" found that multicultural awareness does not change significantly with respect to age. Individuals aged 20 to 24 tend to have similar levels of cultural awareness. Cultural socialization and interactions in educational environments contribute to maintaining this consistency in cultural awareness across different age groups. Therefore, age does not seem to be a determining factor in the development of multicultural awareness. According to research done by Pate, R. H., & Bondi, A. M. (1992) on the topic, "Religious beliefs and practice: An integral aspect of multicultural awareness" found that Multicultural awareness is an ability and understanding that may be grown and improved at any age through experience and education.

According to the study done by Xu et al., (2023) on the topic "Generational gaps in attitudes toward migrants: Hong Kong and Shanghai in comparison" found that Hong Kong's youth are more hostile to immigrants, Shanghai's young people have a greater acceptance of them. The research emphasises how local factors affect how distinct generations see immigration. It points out that younger Shanghai generations, who have more life satisfaction and higher levels of education, are usually inclined to approve of immigrants, while problems with identity promote prejudice against immigrants in Hong Kong. The study underlines how crucial local settings are to comprehending generational disparities in perceptions of immigration.

According to a study done by Dražanová, L., et al (2023) on the topic "Which individual- level factors explain public attitudes toward immigration? a meta-analysis" found that age and immigration attitudes are negatively correlated. In comparison with the younger participants, older respondents had significantly greater anti-immigration attitudes. A person's economic situation is also associated with good attitudes towards immigration; greater income and high-skill occupations both strongly predict positive attitudes towards immigrants. Pro-immigration attitudes are positively correlated with living in an urban area, maybe in part because people in urban areas choose to live in cities and have greater contact with others. Age-related changes in multicultural awareness can be caused by a variety of factors, including life events, exposure to diversity, and generational gaps. In comparison to earlier generations who might have grown up in more similar circumstances, younger generations often display higher levels of multicultural awareness since they often have access to more different settings and school curriculum which encourage diversity.

Same as gender, with respect to age also has less evidence to support its impact on multicultural awareness. There are some studies which shows the lack multicultural awareness in old age people due to various such as lack of exposure due to no migration, lack of knowledge, conservative thoughts and traditions taught in their early age and so on.

Conclusion

Multicultural awareness, as a professional such as psychologists and other profession which work with human is a basic quality. For instance, APA adopts new multicultural guidelines in 2018 for psychologists (APA, 2018, January 1). Three interrelated aspects of human existence can be observed in multiculturalism. First, people's identities and behaviours are influenced by the cultures in which they are nurtured. Second, no culture can accurately represent every aspect of human existence; instead, it is able to represent some part of human experience. Third, there are differences within cultures since all cultures are by nature multiple and diverse (Safdar et al., 2023). It is crucial for psychologists and researchers to recognise and deal with cultural bias in their work as well as to pursue cultural competency and sensitivity in their professional conduct (Na, 2021, March 17). In conclusion, fostering diversity, inclusiveness, and successful communication requires both the development of multicultural awareness. Also fostering multicultural education would help in promoting multicultural awareness in people irrespective of age and gender.

References

American Psychological Association. (2018, January 1). APA adopts new multicultural guidelines. Monitor on Psychology, 49(1). Retrieved from- https://www.apa.org/monitor/2018/01/multicultural-guidelines

APA Dictionary of Psychology. (n.d). https://dictionary.apa.org/culture

APA Dictionary of Psychology. (n.d.-e). https://dictionary.apa.org/multicultural-education

APA Dictionary of Psychology. (n.d.-f). https://dictionary.apa.org/multicultural-psychology

Arts & Culture Council of Strathcona County - 8 Reasons Why Multiculturalism is Important. (n.d.). https://www.accsc.ca/Blog/13205153

D'Andrea, M. (1995). using computer technology to promote multicultural awareness among elementary school-age students. Elementary School Guidance & Counseling, 30(1), 45–54. Rerieved from - http://www.jstor.org/stable/42871191

De Francisco, V. L. (2008, December 18). Deborah Tannen, You just don't understand: Women and men in conversation. New York: William Morrow & Co., 1990. Pp. 330. | Language in Society | Cambridge Core. Cambridge Core. Retrieved from - https://doi.org/10.1017/S0047404500015372

Dražanová, L., Gonnot, J., Heidland, T., & Krüger, F. (2023). Which individual-level factors explain public attitudes toward immigration? a meta-analysis. Journal of Ethnic and Migration Studies, 50(2), 317–340. https://doi.org/10.1080/1369183X.2023.2265576

Foley, R. A., & Lahr, M. M. (2011). The evolution of the diversity of cultures. Philosophical Transactions - Royal Society. Biological Sciences, 366(1567), 1080–1089. https://doi.org/10.1098/rstb.2010.0370

Gudykunst, W. B., & Nishida, T. (2001). Anxiety, uncertainty, and perceived effectiveness of communication across relationships and cultures. International Journal of Intercultural Relations, 25(1), 55-71. https://www.sciencedirect.com/science/article/pii/S0147176700000420

Gudykunst, W.B. and Kim, Y.Y. (2003) Communicating With Strangers an Approach to Intercultural Communication. 4th Edition, McGraw-Hill, Boston. https://www.goingglobalu.com/uploads/7/1/4/2/7142705/gudykunst_ch2_communicat ing_with_strangers 1_.pdf

Hanberger, A. (2010). Multicultural Awareness in Evaluation: Dilemmas and Challenges. Evaluation, 16(2), 177–191. Retrieved from- https://doi.org/10.1177/1356389010361561

Kendra Cherry. (2022, April 6). Psychology Explains How Cultural Differences Influence Human Behavior. Verywell Mind. Retrieved from- https://www.verywellmind.com/what-is-cross-cultural-psychology-2794903

Libretexts. (2024, April 3). 3.2: History of Evolution of Multiculturalism in the United States. Workforce LibreTexts. https://workforce.libretexts.org/Bookshelves/Corrections/Community_and_the_Justice_System_(Wymore_and_Raber)

Na. (2019, February). What do we mean by "culture"? Hofstede Insights news. https://news.hofstede-insights.com/news/what-do-we-mean-by-culture

Na. (2021, March 17). Psychology Hub. Cultural Bias In Psychology. Retrieved from- https://www.psychologyhub.co.uk/culture-bias-in-psychology/

Na. (Nd). Unit 4 evolution of Multicultural - Egyankosh. UNIT-4 EVOLUTION OF MULTICULTURAL SOCIETY. https://egyankosh.ac.in/bitstream/123456789/20831/1/Unit-4.pdf

Pate, R. H., & Bondi, A. M. (1992). Religious beliefs and practice: An integral aspect of multicultural awareness. Counselor Education and Supervision, 32(2), 108–115. Retrieved from- https://doi.org/10.1002/j.1556-6978.1992.tb00180.x

Phinney, J. S., & Chavira, V. (1995). Parental ethnic socialization and adolescent coping with problems related to ethnicity. Journal of Research on Adolescence, 5(1), 31–53. Retrieved from- https://doi.org/10.1207/s15327795jra0501_2

Ponce, A. (2017). Gender and Anti-immigrant Attitudes in Europe. Socius, 3. https://doi.org/10.1177/2378023117729970

Safdar, S., Mahali, S. C., & Scott, C. (2023). A critical review of multiculturalism and interculturalism as integration frameworks: The case of Canada. International Journal of Intercultural Relations, 93, 101756. https://doi.org/10.1016/j.ijintrel.2023.101756

Schalk-Soekar, S. R., Van De Vijver, F. J., & Hoogsteder, M. (2004). Attitudes toward multiculturalism of immigrants and majority members in the Netherlands. International Journal of Intercultural Relations, 28(6), 533–550. https://doi.org/10.1016/j.ijintrel.2005.01.009 (https://www.sciencedirect.com/science/article/pii/S0147176705000118)

Sipuan, M. I. (2022). HISTORY OF MULTICULTURALISM. In European Journal of Research Development and Sustainability (EJRDS) (Vols. 3–3, Issue 6, pp. 41–42). https://www.scholarzest.com /https://scholarzest.com/index.php/ejrds/article/ download/2309/1911/4354

Xu, C., Gu, P., Zhang, Z., Xu, M., & Li, J. (2023). Generational gaps in attitudes toward migrants: Hong Kong and Shanghai in comparison. International Journal of Intercultural Relations, 95, 101829. https://doi.org/ 10.1016/j.ijintrel.2023.101829

Yusri, F., & Afrida, Y. (2022). The differences of cultural awareness based on gender, age, race, and region of the students. Konselor, 11(4), 152-161. doi: https://doi.org/ 10.24036/02022114119545-0-00

CHAPTER SEVENTEEN

Interwoven Realities: Pop Culture and Media in Modern Society

- **Nikitha M K**

Background

Mass culture has primarily changed the relationship between the mass media and the pop icons. Popular culture closely ties to media in the form of television shows, music, and films. The digital age has brought about an extensive or rapid development or evolution in the field of pop culture, which is viewed more as a vibrant element of a stand-alone technological society. Media influence in the procreation and continuity of pop culture is not only massive but also complex. Traditionally, media have been the key actors in moving cultures into the future. Culture is not a static concept but cannot be directly appropriated by media alone, as culture is also changing, thus learning a distribution of media (Muhren,2017). Media serves as a tool to help the industry manage to keep the message of pop culture alive. These technologies are not just an additional layer, but material entities that help fashion social and cultural identity and the popular culture has consequently been applied with technology. Curiously, a large part of popular culture that arises on TV and in the movies and on digital platforms is actually the result of the aforenamed societal conditions. There will be an opportunity to build upon continues but it will only take a successful attempt, such as surveys and adaptation of the current landscape to make it happen. Popular culture is a living expression of the citizens' lives in a community, of which media serve as a channel for the society. Exploring consumerism as a non-effectual action of isolation that leads to separation and the object v holding careless disdain speaks to losing craft labour and engaging customers and art as cheap mass production acts as a warning to this modern lifestyle. Media in all its aspects have left no stone in the society untouched and the presence of it in shaping culture can only be echoed to a varying degree in the way films and other pop elements become transformation parts. On the other hand, forms of media e.g., TV and films have been platforms of the ideological hegemony of the USA while keeping the interest of the audience abroad due to the fact that American media tends to promote the central values of their culture globally (Anderson, 2014).Research has confirmed that the popular culture has been transformed into a solid feature within the digital age of media. Based on the information given in the opening sentence of the article, this study will examine how the media is the main tool for spreading and promoting popular culture. It also notes the cultural changes that happened due to urbanization and the advancement of technology. The available body of literature over the past quarter of a century has undoubtedly been critically analysed in this respect. Furthermore, this article demonstrates a multitude of pop culture components such as such films, TV shows, online video games, politics, music, sports, promotions, e-commerce, & mobile applications and argues through the media's critical role in popularizing and promoting it. Through the discovery of this study, what the media has been influencing the most, would be cultural and pop culture. This study also suggests the prevalence of pop culture as a tool for controlling the agenda and cultural diplomacy, which, in turn, will be used for the promotion of the development and resourcefulness of nations, and people. Though it is constantly changing, pop culture, which also receives the backing via the media, remains a core element of its promotion.

The scope of studies investigating the connection between society and the media is broadening. The inexorable spread of multimedia in our lives has become an unavoidable fact. As a result, media has a significant impact on every element of life and society. Being a member of the discourse's world has altered and continues to transform our entire way of life. This entire manner of living is referred to as culture. According to researchers, in our mediatized environment, the media acts and plays a critical role in moulding culture and the society. Similar to this, contend that we live in a media-saturated world where the media influences us on a personal as well as a social level and has woven itself into our cultural identity. In this vein, a lot of study has shown how the media affects and influences a variety of spheres of life, including daily living as well as fashion, sports, agriculture, internet marketing, tourism, show business, etc.

The various facets of the changing interaction among both the media and society that subsequently results in cultural change have also been studied in research. The role that a media play in pop culture is a fascinating topic in the study of culture and media, especially in light of past studies. Further research and debate are necessary in this area given the significance of the subject. This essay examines Modern Culture (Pop Culture) in particular and offers a fresh perspective on the connection amongst pop culture and the media. This review article defines culture, chronicles the division of cultures like High, Folk, and Pop Culture, as well as cultural paradigm alterations after the Industrial Revolution that helped us better comprehend Popular Culture (and its emergence). In order to highlight the crucial contribution that media makes in promoting and developing pop culture, the current study covers a variety of mediatized aspects of popular culture, including films, TV shows, online video games, politics, music, sports, commercials, e-commerce, and mobile applications. This study offers further prospective perspectives to demonstrate the value and influence of popular culture as well as the critical function of the media.

Review of Literature

If we have this theory about what culture is, we can grasp popular culture better. Culture has been described in a variety of ways from various angles, taking socio-geographical and normative factors into account. As an illustration, Kuper (2001) describes many concepts of culture, such as the romantic German concept of "Kultur,—which give out with religion, language, and national identity, and the French Enlightenment's idea of culture as a quest for perfection and advancement on a global scale. In contrast, the conflict between the rich and the poor, the middle class, and the working class, is central to British societal perspectives on culture. The American idea describes culture as a whole way of life. There are several perspectives on culture (Storey, 2021).

According to Spencer-Oatey (2021), culture is an ill-defined set of customs, norms, values, perspectives, and social agreements that everyone shares and that have an impact on both an individual's conduct and how they perceive the behavior of others. In a different research, Spencer-Oatey (2012) defines the characteristics of culture by combining numerous concepts. Culture, according to Spenser-Oatey, has several levels. It may be learnt at the social and personal levels and is a gradual process. This is a comprehensive way of life that encompasses a wide range of things, such as daily activities, ways of living, traditions, values, foods, modes of entertainment, etc. It is also important to note that this way of life can be related to factors such as gender, age, ethnicity, organizational ties, and national identity.

Culture in a civilization may be divided primarily into three categories: intellectual culture, folk culture, and pop culture (popular culture). The books and behaviors that are regarded as exclusive or of the highest caliber are referred to as high culture. High culture includes activities like opera, horse racing, ballet, golf, gallery art, and literary works like Shakespeare. The specialized elite elements of society adopt high culture and can afford it (Delaney, 2007). Debnath (2019), in a similar vein, asserts that "high culture is a collection of ideas, beliefs, thoughts, trends, practices, and works—intellectual or creative-that is designed for refined, cultured, and educated elite people" (p.274).

Folk culture, on the other hand, is a regional, local, rural, and basic culture. Folk culture discourages innovation and new trends, which makes it conservative (Delaney, 2007).

It endures and is passed down the years, as is the case with customary foods, regional practices, attire, folk music, etc. High and folk cultures share two elements that are created and consumed on an exceedingly small scale by the affluent and working classes, respectively. By separating folk culture from pop culture, Nestor Garca-Canclini (1995; referenced in Kraidy, 2019) contends that neither traditional culture nor popular culture is affected negatively by cultural advancements.

Crossman (2019), in a similar spirit, emphasizes that the word "Popular Culture" was first used in the 19th century and that it refers to the media that the majority of society consumes, such as music, art, literature, design, dance, cinema, cyber culture, television, etc. The researcher continues by stating that sometimes strong forces use pop culture as a tool to repress the general populace in order to accomplish their goals. Nevertheless, Stewart Hall (1998; as referenced in Kraidy, 2019) of the British school of class system theory solely sees popular culture as a persistent force opposing the dominant culture.

Pop culture was influenced by the industrial revolution. Pop culture is viewed by many academics as an outcome of industrialization and urbanization. One thing is certain, however— and Parker (2011) cites this as an example—pop culture evolved immediately following industrialization and urbanization. The industrial revolution, which started around the end of the 18th century, significantly altered society's outlook while also sparking urbanization and technical advancement. People began to move from rural to urban regions as a means of creativity and advancement. This was when folk culture gave way to pop culture. Individuals from various rural communities and origins began residing together and adopting certain lifestyle practices. Given these conditions, commercialization, mass manufacturing consumption, and the formation of a business sector and corporate social culture.

Popular culture serves as a social bond for people with shared interests and is promoted by corporations in order to achieve their financial goals (Dolby, 2003). According to Kraidy (2019), popular culture is a byproduct of modern capitalism and an industrialized product that was intended to reeducate people so that they could fit into the capitalist model of economics. It is a dynamic process that is ongoing rather than static. Pop culture may therefore be explained in a variety of ways. It is a culture that is widely accepted by society and is mass produced and consumed. Also, it depicts a cultural conflict between the upper and lower classes. It is necessary to exist in capitalism and serves the business sector.

Sources of Pop-culture

Mass media is an influential force, and the development of digital media has increased its influence and strength. After the rise of mass media and technology communication methods, there occurred a profound shift in culture. Culture has been created and supported by the media. The media strongly influences both our culture and daily life. A culture that is increasingly mediated includes print, graphic, audiovisual, and digital mediatization. Pop culture is shaped through media use, which is directly related to societal change. Mediatized culture is the term used to describe a society that relies heavily on the media (Fornäs, 2014). So-called "mediatized sources of pop culture" are sources of popular culture that rely on the media.

These sources serve as authentic representations of popular culture that are widely embraced and consumed by the majority of the population. Given how dependent pop culture is on the media, it is necessary to explore these mediatized origins of pop culture in order to illuminate how the media shapes and propagates pop culture. Films, TV shows, online games, politics, music, sports, ads, e-commerce, and mobile apps are examples of mediated sources of pop culture.

Films

Movies have been crucial to the development of popular culture. They have a significant influence and reach in a variety of social sectors and are extensively produced and viewed on a national and worldwide scale. Individuals from diverse demographic groups began residing together and adopting the speech patterns, wardrobe choices, and conduct of their shared idols on the big screen (Libraries, 2010). Although movies are not trustworthy sources of information, according to Rose (2007), films may nonetheless be useful in explaining and teaching specific biological ideas, such as animal evolutionary, cloning, genetics, etc. Movies have the power to alter people's perceptions as well. For instance, Febrina (2019) stated that America accentuated a select character in Japanese-adapted films that altered how the public perceived characters.

For contrast, Hachi (a devoted dog) changed people's perceptions of dogs, and numerous goods subsequently included devoted dogs in their marketing. Also, Godzilla was portrayed as an American persona and seen as the nation's savior. Movies have been utilized and demands of the business politically, socially, and commercially, as Elezaj (2019) recalled, and Adolf Hitler utilized movies as propaganda during the Second World War as one example of this. He added that films influence culture, educate history, raise awareness, and inspire. Hollywood movies are contributing to cultural imperialism, according to research on the cultural effects of cinematic media. These films have a significant impact on Pakistani youth's attitudes and moral standards in addition to promoting western culture in that country.

Similar to this, Jones (2018) discussed socially significant films in a different article. For instance, Crazy Rich Asians emphasized the issue of interpretation and the class structure. The topic of racism was underlined in Green Book; A Private War brought attention to the problem of war, Shoplifters to the problem of poverty, 3 Identical Strangers to the problem of medical ethics and psychological wellbeing, The Hatred You Give to the problem of police misbehavior, and Black Panther to the problem of colonialism and technology.

TV Programs

A significant source for pop culture is television. These include conversation programmers, dramas, reality TV, cuisine shows, fashion shows, morning shows, etc. TV shows have a significant impact on both domestic and foreign media. The media exaggerated the impact of the Panama Leaks. There was a profusion of political and media debate. Up until it led to the overthrow of several political regimes and shocked the political establishment, it was the topic of every political discussion show. Reality Television has also made a significant impact. Reality TV shows were defined by researchers as programs that include genuine individuals showcasing their talents for the audience.

Zhao (2018) concludes that reality TV programs may affect & encourage national politics, ideology, economics, and policymaking by using the example of the singing competition Super Voice Girl (SVG). SVG introduced the idea of queer and set it apart from lesbian, which was well-received in the entertainment sector. Reality TV programs with high viewership like The Voice, America's Got Talent, Dance India Dance, and India Got Talent build heroes from nothing. Although fashion events highlight and influence societal fashion trends, cooking shows alter and improve our relationship with food. TV dramas have a big cultural effect as well. The Turkish play Ertugrul Ghazi is the pinnacle of popular culture with a global audience. Pakistani dramas are very clearly influencing the culture of the country.

Online Gaming

Digital media fostered real-life encounters in the form of online games as a consequence of technological advancements. A video game is a multimedia game that may be played on computers and mobile phones, among other things. Reid (2014) argues that in this evolved era, video games have assimilated into mainstream culture. Online gamers enjoy themselves by earning awards and admiration for accomplishments that contribute to their feeling successful. Young people love to play online games. For instance, study revealed that 75% of young people in South Korea are addicted to internet gaming. The previous two decades have seen significant growth in the video game business.

According to a survey by the Entertainment Software Association (2021), 227 million Americans of all ages and genders, who surged over the Covid-19 period, play video games. Richter (2020) points out that in 2019, the videogame sector generated $145.7 billion in income, outpacing the box office and music sectors, which generated $42.5 billion and $20.2 billion in sales, respectively. Only in the USA, the PC game market generated $37 billion in sales in 2020, while the mobile gaming market generated $77 billion (Clement, 2021). There is a tone of studies on the advantages of gaming's development as well as the psychological effects of video games and health risks. Statistics and the volume of consumption shed information on internet gaming as popular culture.

Music

One of the sectors with the fastest growth rates worldwide is music. Celebrities and media figures are the vocalists. Hollander (2010) attributed this celebrity cult phenomenon to the emergence of pop culture following the passing of Michael Jackson, which for days eclipsed all other programmers and news articles. Hollander continues by arguing that modern music is a fusion of several styles that is viewed as a component of a common culture. Hollywood musicians have numerous millionaires and social media followers, making them well-known internationally.

One common method of fostering cultural interchange is the acceptance of singers from one culture or geographic area by another (for example English singers in Bollywood and vice versa and also Pakistani singers singing for Bollywood). Due to its widespread consumption and success as a global source of entertainment, music serves as a foundation for popular culture. There are several online and mobile music resources available, including YouTube, and best songs, Deezer, Soundcloud, Spotify, etc.

Advertisements

Pop culture involves commercialization, as was already noted. It has manufacturing, consumption, and reproduction processes. Advertising plays a crucial role in quickening this process in the period of marketing. The lifeblood of the media when it comes of generating cash is advertising. This is acknowledged as the most effective method of persuasion and promotion. Advertising has an impact on people, as well as new social trends that lead to cultural change. As was already noted, the British conception of popular culture is founded on social strata and the pursuit of compatibility. The lower class is encouraged to battle with the higher class.

Advertisements encourage people to fit in with society. For instance, slim is portrayed as the perfect image of themselves for women, which encourages body dissatisfaction. Advertisements encourage women to use various things to modify their bodies (Bloom Ads, 2021). Multinational advertising has entered the market as commercialization has grown along with globalization. Transnational firms create in bulk for global consumption, and then promote their products globally. Such marketing has a measurable impact on culture. According to research by Ochonogor & Nwachukwu (2019), the Coca-Cola advertising campaign had an impact on Nigerian adolescents by altering their prejudices in daily life. Advertising is a significant component of pop culture due to the numerous advertising campaigns, numerous advertisements, and massive consumption.

Pop Culture and Cultural Diplomacy

Some academics have asserted that pop culture can be exploited in the future for transnational agenda shaping and cultural imperialism through observation of the influence of media-supported pop culture. Jung (2019), citing the Korean cultural wave, suggests that media may be utilized to define cultural agendas through pop culture. The study asserts further that this application of pop culture, also known as pop culture politics and soft power, may change how the global public perceives any particular country (Iwabuchi, 2015). In a similar vein, Sawada (2016) describes how proponents of pop culture diplomacy link it to soft power, cultural diplomacy, and public diplomacy. According to the study, pop culture diplomacy is cultural diplomacy that primarily draws on popular culture.

Conclusion

Considering the examined literature, it is determined that pop culture refers to anything that is created, utilized, consumed, viewed, and followed on a big scale by the public. This study backs up the mediatization theory's assertions that media has altered culture and increased society's reliance on the media. The media has been crucial in fostering cultural change and continues to be a major force in shaping and advancing popular culture. Pop culture and the media are closely related, dependent, and bonded. It may be argued that media and pop culture complement one another when the previously described intertextual sources of popular culture are taken into consideration.

The media is being employed as a mediator, player, and facilitator across all sources of popular culture. Since pop culture is a constantly changing procedure, the media always will play a significant role in it. This is because journalistic sources of pop culture are growing as a result of technological advancements in the media industry, and because these sources are also having a significant impact on society and its culture through their high levels of consumption.

Media is a potent agent for social and cultural shifts since media platforms and users are both growing at the exact same time. Further study in this field is required due to developments within the media sector, cultural shifts, and growing media dependence. With the rise and accessibility of the media, pop culture has become a powerful force on a worldwide and national scale that will only grow in the future. Because we live in an era of big data and datafication, there will be additional aspects of the issue to investigate.

References

Baker, A. (2020, February 7). The Most Watched Sporting Events in The World - Roadtrips. https://www.roadtrips.com/blog/the most-watched-sporting-events-in-the world/ Bhatti, A., Akram, H.,

Basit, H. M., Khan, A. U., Mahwish, S., Naqvi, R., & Bilal, M. (2020). E-commerce trends during COVID-19 Pandemic. International Journal of Future Generation Communication and Networking, 13(2), 1449–1452.

Biegun, J., Edgerton, J. D., & Roberts, L. W. (2021). Measuring Problem Online Video Gaming and Its Association With Problem Gambling and Suspected Motivational, Mental Health, and Behavioral Risk Factors in a Sample of University Students. Games and Culture, 16(4), 434–456. https://doi.org/10.1177/155541201989752 4

Bloom Ads. (2021). How Pop Culture Impacts Your Advertising. https://blog.bloomads.com/blog/how pop-culture-impacts-your-advertising

Clement, J. (2021, April 29). Video game industry - Statistics & Facts | Statista. https://www.statista.com/topics/868/vid eo-games/

Coban, F. (2016). The Role of the Media in International Relations: From the CNN Effect to the Al –Jazeere Effect. Journal of International Relations and Foreign Policy, 4(2), 45–61. https://doi.org/10.15640/jirfp.v4n2a3

Crossman, A. (2019, December 9). The Definition of Marriage in Sociology. ThoughtCo. https://www.thoughtco.com/marriage 3026396

Delaney, T. (2007). Pop Culture: An Overview | Issue 64 | Philosophy Now. https://philosophynow.org/issues/64/Po p_Culture_An_Overview

Kim, A. J., & Ko, E. (2010). Impacts of luxury fashion brand's social media marketing on customer relationship and purchase intention. Journal of Global Fashion Marketing, 1(3), 164–171. https://doi.org/10.1080/20932685.2010.1 0593068

Manangi, S. (2017, August 1). Uber's global expansion strategy - —Think local to expand globall – will it work for startups? | LinkedIn. https://www.linkedin.com/pulse/ubers global- expansion-strategy-think-local expand-work-manangi/

Morris, W., & James, P. (2017). Social media, an entrepreneurial opportunity for agriculture- based enterprises. Journal of Small Business and Enterprise Development, 24(4), 1028– 1045. https://doi.org/10.1108/JSBED-01-2017- 0018

Rose, C. S. (2007). Biology in the movies: Using the double-edged sword of popular culture to enhance public understanding of science. Evolutionary Biology, 34(1–2), 49–54. https://doi.org/10.1007/s11692- 007-9001-8

Spencer-Oatey, H. (2021). British and Chinese Reactions to Compliment Responses. In Culturally Speaking Second Edition (Second). Continuum. https://doi.org/10.5040/9781350934085. ch-005

Storey, J. (2021). Cultural Theory and Popular Culture: An Introduction. In Cultural Theory and Popular Culture: An Introduction. Taylor and Francis. https://doi.org/10.4324/9781003011729

Street, J. (2020). Popular culture and political communication. Comunicazione Politica, 21(1), 129–140.

https://doi.org/10.3270/96428

Williams, R. H., & Kuper, A. (2001). Culture: The Anthropologists' Account. Contemporary Sociology, 30(3), 302. https://doi.org/10.2307/3089289

Yang, L. (2014). Reality talent shows in China. In L. Ouellette (Ed.), Academia.edu (516– 540). John Wiley & Sons, Inc. https://www.academia.edu/download/40502071/Reality_Talent_Shows_in_China .pdf

CHAPTER EIGHTEEN

Empathy and Judgment: Perceptions of Rape Victims

- **Dibyashree Panda**

Background

The attitudes towards rape victims in India are deeply influenced by a complex interplay of historical, cultural, and social factors. India's long history is marked by diverse cultural and religious traditions, many of which have shaped gender roles and societal norms in ways that are still evident today. Historically, the patriarchal structure of Indian society has positioned women in subordinate roles, leading to deeply ingrained beliefs about gender and sexuality. These traditional beliefs have often resulted in the stigmatization and victim-blaming of rape victims, perpetuating a culture where victims of sexual violence are ostracized and their experiences minimized.

In modern India, the landscape is gradually shifting due to increased awareness and advocacy efforts. High-profile cases and extensive media coverage have brought the issue of sexual violence into the public eye, sparking widespread outrage and calls for justice. Despite these advancements, societal attitudes towards rape victims remain largely unchanged. Victims frequently face severe social ostracism, and the media, while instrumental in raising awareness, often perpetuates harmful stereotypes and misinformation. This creates a challenging environment for victims who seek justice and support.

A cross-cultural perspective reveals that these issues are not unique to India. In many Western countries, movements like feminism and #MeToo have significantly altered public discourse around sexual violence, leading to more supportive attitudes and stronger legal frameworks. However, issues of victim-blaming and stigmatization persist globally, albeit in varying degrees. In some cultures, gender and sexuality norms are even more rigid, resulting in harsher societal reactions to rape victims. These cross-cultural comparisons highlight both the progress made and the challenges that remain in addressing sexual violence worldwide (Larsen & Long, 1988).

The psychological impact of rape on victims is profound and far-reaching. In India, the additional burden of societal stigma exacerbates mental health issues such as depression, anxiety, and post-traumatic stress disorder (PTSD). Victims often struggle with feelings of shame and isolation, which can hinder their recovery and reintegration into society. The support systems available to rape victims in India, including legal recourse, medical assistance, and social services, are often inadequate. Resource constraints, bureaucratic hurdles, and societal prejudices pose significant barriers to accessing these services, leaving many victims without the support they need.

The present chapter tries to unpack the complex interplay of factors which give birth to such attitudes by exploring the attitudes toward rape victims across different cultural contexts in India. We must be optimistic that strategies can be made to avert these abuses and that support will be extended to its victims by understanding the cross-cultural variations. This chapter will emphasize the necessity of proposing a much more nuanced contribution that integrates the different cultural contexts of India so that the final output may be more inclusive and supportive of all victims of sexual violence.

Cross-cultural Framework within India

India is a land of immense cultural diversity, with a myriad of languages, religions, castes, and regional identities coexisting within its borders. This diversity profoundly influences attitudes and beliefs, including those towards rape victims. Understanding the cross-cultural framework within India requires an appreciation of how these different cultural contexts shape societal norms and behaviors.

In urban areas, for instance, exposure to global media and progressive movements often results in more liberal attitudes towards gender and sexuality. Cities like Mumbai, Delhi, and Bangalore, which are hubs of economic and social activity, tend to have populations that are more open to discussions about sexual violence and more supportive of victims. However, even within these urban centers, there are significant pockets of conservative thought influenced by traditional values. In contrast, rural areas often adhere more strictly to traditional norms. Here, patriarchal values are deeply entrenched, and gender roles are more rigidly defined. This can result in harsher stigmatization of rape victims, who are often seen as bringing shame to their families and communities. In these settings, the lack of anonymity and close-knit community structures can make it incredibly difficult for victims to speak out or seek help.

Caste dynamics add another layer of complexity. The caste system, though officially abolished, still significantly impacts social interactions and attitudes. Victims from lower castes may face double discrimination: both for their caste and for being victims of sexual violence. In some cases, upper-caste perpetrators of rape go unpunished due to the power dynamics at play, further perpetuating a culture of impunity and silence.

Religion also plays a crucial role in shaping attitudes. India is home to multiple religions, each with its own set of beliefs and practices concerning gender and sexuality. In some religious communities, there might be a strong emphasis on purity and honor, leading to greater stigmatization of rape victims. Conversely, other communities might offer more support and understanding, grounded in their religious teachings of compassion and justice.

In India, rape accounts for about 12% of all crimes against women. The number of reported instances is spread out rather unevenly across the country. In India, there are approximately 6.3 reported rape cases for every 100,000 people. This conceals significant geographic disparities, with Tamil Nadu having a rate of less than one and Sikkim having rates of 30.3 and 22.5, respectively. Of the 19 metro areas in the nation, Kolkata has the fewest incidences of sexual assault against women, according to the most recent NCRB data. According to news agency PTI, Coimbatore in Tamil Nadu has also not recorded any cases of sexual harassment. States like Tamil Nadu, Kerala, and Andhra Pradesh are last on the list, while Uttar Pradesh (59,853) has the most criminal cases involving women. Rajasthan

(41,550) comes in right after Maharashtra (37,144), which comes in second. The record shows that nearly 2,000 more rapes were reported in the north than in the south in 2011, according to information from the National Crime Records Bureau. According to a report in The Wall Street Journal titled Authors of Statistics: Rape Conviction Rates Throughout India, campaigners play down the notion that one section of the country is intrinsically safer for women than another (Singh, 2017).

Global Perspectives

While the focus of this chapter is on the diverse cultural landscape within India, it is useful to briefly consider global perspectives to provide a comparative context. Globally, attitudes towards rape victims vary widely, influenced by cultural, legal, and social factors. In many Western countries, feminist movements have significantly shaped public discourse on sexual violence, leading to greater awareness and more supportive attitudes towards victims. The #MeToo movement, for instance, has had a profound impact worldwide, encouraging victims to speak out and demanding accountability from perpetrators. In countries like Sweden and Canada, strong legal frameworks and progressive social policies provide robust support for rape victims. These countries often have comprehensive systems in place, including counseling, legal aid, and medical care, aimed at helping victims recover and seek justice. Public education campaigns also play a crucial role in changing societal attitudes, promoting the message that rape is a crime for which the perpetrator, not the victim, is responsible (Beckman et al, 1990).

However, issues of victim-blaming and stigmatization are not exclusive to India. In many parts of the world, victims of rape still face significant challenges. Cultural norms in some societies, particularly those with strong patriarchal traditions, can result in severe stigmatization and ostracism of rape victims. In such contexts, victims may be pressured to remain silent or even forced to marry their rapists to "restore" family honor.

Understanding these global perspectives helps highlight both the progress and the persistent challenges in addressing sexual violence. It underscores the importance of cultural sensitivity and the need for tailored approaches that consider the unique contexts within each society. For India, this means acknowledging the vast cultural diversity within its borders and addressing the specific needs and challenges of different communities to create a more supportive environment for rape victims. (Olszewska, Piotrowski & Wojciechowski, 2022).

Historical Perspectives on Gender and Sexual Violence

India's history is a tapestry of diverse cultures, religions, and social structures, all of which have influenced attitudes towards gender and sexual violence. Ancient Indian society, as reflected in texts like the Vedas and epics such as the Mahabharata and Ramayana, had complex views on gender. Women were often revered and depicted as powerful figures in mythology. However, these texts also reflect a patriarchal society where women's roles were largely confined to the domestic sphere.

In ancient times, practices like Sati (the self-immolation of widows) and child marriage were prevalent, reflecting a societal obsession with female purity and honor. Women were expected to maintain the honor of their families, and any deviation from this ideal could lead to severe consequences, including violence. These practices were rooted in the belief that a woman's worth was intrinsically tied to her chastity and obedience.

During the medieval period, the status of women further deteriorated with the advent of various invaders and the establishment of feudal systems. The Mughal era, for example, saw the enforcement of Purdah (seclusion of women) and a rise in practices like honor killings. Women's autonomy was severely restricted, and they were often treated as property. Sexual violence was used as a tool of control and subjugation, both within and outside marriage.

The British colonial period brought about some changes with the introduction of modern legal systems and reforms. The British administration enacted laws to abolish practices like Sati and child marriage, and to provide women with some legal rights. However, these reforms were often limited and faced significant resistance from traditionalists. The colonial period also saw the rise of social reform movements, led by figures like Raja Ram Mohan Roy and Ishwar Chandra Vidyasagar, who advocated for women's rights and education. Despite these efforts, the overall societal attitude towards women and sexual violence remained deeply patriarchal.

Influence of Traditional Gender Roles and Patriarchal Norms

Traditional gender roles in India have long been influenced by patriarchal norms, which dictate a rigid division of responsibilities and power between men and women. Men are typically seen as the breadwinners and protectors, while women are expected to be homemakers and caregivers. These roles are reinforced through cultural practices, religious teachings, and social expectations, creating a framework that often subjugates women.

Patriarchal norms also place a heavy emphasis on female chastity and modesty. A woman's worth is often measured by her ability to conform to these ideals, and any deviation is met with harsh judgment. This creates a culture where victims of sexual violence are blamed and shamed, rather than supported. The concept of family honor is intricately linked to the behavior and sexuality of women, leading to practices that control and monitor their actions from a young age.

In rural areas, where traditional norms are more rigidly adhered to, the control over women's sexuality is even more pronounced. Practices like dowry, which commodify women as financial burdens, and honor killings, which punish perceived transgressions, continue to reflect deeply ingrained patriarchal values. These norms not only perpetuate gender inequality but also contribute to a culture of silence and victim-blaming around sexual violence

Evolution of Societal Attitudes Over Time

Societal attitudes towards gender and sexual violence in India have evolved, particularly in the past few decades. The independence movement in the early 20th century marked a significant shift, as it brought about a wave of social and political change. Women played active roles in the struggle for independence, and leaders like Mahatma Gandhi advocated for women's rights and empowerment.

Post-independence, the Indian Constitution granted equal rights to women and men, marking a formal commitment to gender equality. However, the translation of these legal rights into societal attitudes has been slow and uneven. The feminist movement in India gained momentum in the 1970s and 1980s, bringing issues of domestic violence, dowry deaths, and sexual harassment into the public discourse. Activists and organizations worked tirelessly to challenge patriarchal norms and advocate for legal reforms.

High-profile cases of sexual violence, such as the Mathura rape case in 1972 and the Delhi gang rape in 2012, have sparked widespread outrage and led to significant legal and societal changes. The Mathura case, where a young tribal girl was raped by policemen, highlighted the issue of custodial rape and led to amendments in rape laws. The Delhi gang rape case, which involved the brutal assault and murder of a young woman on a bus, resulted in nationwide protests and the formation of the Justice Verma Committee, which recommended comprehensive changes to laws on sexual violence.

Legal reforms have been instrumental in addressing sexual violence. Laws such as the Protection of Women from Domestic Violence Act (2005) and the Criminal Law (Amendment) Act (2013) have strengthened legal protections for women and expanded the definitions of sexual violence. However, the implementation of these laws varies, and many victims still face significant barriers to justice, including stigma, lack of legal awareness, and systemic biases within law enforcement and the judiciary. Education and economic empowerment are key factors in transforming societal attitudes. Access to education for girls and women has improved, and more women are entering the workforce, challenging traditional gender roles. These changes are gradually shifting perceptions about women's capabilities and rights, contributing to a more equitable society.

Cultural Diversity and Attitudes

India's vast and varied geography encompasses a multitude of cultural identities, each region boasting its own distinct traditions, languages, and social norms. This cultural diversity significantly influences attitudes towards rape victims, creating a complex tapestry of responses across the country.

In Northern India, regions such as Punjab, Haryana, and Uttar Pradesh often exhibit deeply entrenched patriarchal values. In these areas, honor and family reputation are paramount, and any sexual violence incident is seen as a stain on familial honor. Victims are frequently blamed and shamed, further perpetuating their trauma. In rural areas, the lack of anonymity and close-knit community structures can make it particularly difficult for victims to come forward, as they risk ostracization and further violence. Urban centers like Delhi, while somewhat more progressive, still grapple with these traditional views, and societal attitudes can vary widely even within the city (Hetu, 2020).

Southern India, including states like Tamil Nadu, Karnataka, and Kerala, tends to have a slightly more progressive outlook due to higher literacy rates and better gender parity. Kerala, in particular, is noted for its matrilineal traditions in some communities, which historically accorded women more respect and autonomy. However, despite these progressive strides, patriarchal norms are still prevalent, and attitudes towards rape victims can be harsh. In Tamil Nadu, for example, the traditional emphasis on family honor means that victims often face significant societal pressure to remain silent. Yet, urban centers like Bangalore are more open to discussing and addressing issues of sexual violence, thanks in part to a vibrant civil society and media presence.

In Eastern India, states such as West Bengal and Odisha reflect a mix of progressive and traditional attitudes.

Kolkata, the capital of West Bengal, has a rich history of social reform and intellectual discourse, contributing to more supportive attitudes towards rape victims. However, in rural parts of West Bengal and Odisha, traditional norms still hold sway, and victims often face severe stigmatization. Tribal areas in Odisha present another layer of complexity, where customary laws and practices can significantly influence attitudes towards sexual violence, sometimes offering more support to victims, depending on the community.

The Western region of India, including states like Maharashtra, Gujarat, and Rajasthan, presents a diverse picture. Maharashtra's capital, Mumbai, is known for its progressive views and active advocacy groups supporting rape victims. The city's cosmopolitan nature fosters a more open dialogue about sexual violence. In contrast, Rajasthan, with its strong feudal history and deeply rooted patriarchal culture, often sees rape victims facing severe backlash and honor-related violence. Gujarat's attitudes can vary significantly between its urban and rural areas, with cities like Ahmedabad being more progressive than its rural counterparts.

Role of Caste

Caste dynamics play a crucial role in shaping attitudes towards rape victims in India. The caste system, though officially abolished, remains a potent social force. Lower-caste (Dalit) women are disproportionately affected by sexual violence, and their experiences are often overlooked or dismissed by both society and law enforcement.

In many cases, rape is used as a tool of oppression against lower-caste communities, and the perpetrators, who often belong to higher castes, enjoy impunity. The intersection of caste and gender discrimination means that

Dalit women face double marginalization. They are not only stigmatized as rape victims but also further devalued because of their caste status. This creates a climate of fear and silence, where victims are reluctant to come forward due to the perceived futility of seeking justice.

Upper-caste victims, while also facing stigma, may have more resources and social capital to navigate the aftermath of sexual violence. However, the emphasis on family honor and purity means that upper-caste victims are also pressured into silence and face significant societal backlash if they choose to speak out.

Religious Beliefs and Practices

Religious beliefs and practices significantly influence societal views towards rape victims in India, with each major religion imparting distinct teachings that shape attitudes toward gender and sexuality. In Hinduism, which is the predominant religion, ancient texts often revere feminine power through goddesses like Durga and Kali. However, societal practices traditionally emphasize female purity and chastity, leading to the stigmatization of rape victims who are often seen as impure and as tarnishing family honor. Similarly, in Islamic communities, the cultural emphasis on female modesty and family honor can result in severe social repercussions for rape victims, who may be viewed as bringing dishonor to their families. Nevertheless, progressive voices within both Hindu and Muslim communities advocate for victims' rights and challenge traditional norms (Vohra, 2022).

Christianity, Sikhism, and Buddhism in India also offer varied perspectives influenced by both religious teachings and cultural practices. While Christian teachings advocate compassion and support for victims, cultural norms within some Christian communities may still reflect patriarchal attitudes, leading to social stigma. Sikhism, with its emphasis on equality and justice, theoretically provides a supportive framework for rape victims, although cultural practices within Sikh communities can sometimes mirror broader societal norms. Buddhism, though a minority religion, promotes compassion and non-violence, aligning with progressive views on gender and sexual violence. Overall, religious beliefs and practices in India create a complex landscape where victims of sexual violence may either find support or face stigmatization, depending on the dominant religious and cultural context of their communities

Media Portrayal and Public Attitudes

The media plays a powerful role in shaping public perceptions of rape and sexual violence. The portrayal of rape cases in Indian media often reflects and reinforces societal attitudes, both positive and negative. Traditional media, including newspapers and television, frequently highlight the sensational aspects of rape cases, sometimes focusing excessively on the details of the crime or the victim's personal life. This sensationalism can contribute to the objectification of victims and, at times, perpetuate victim-blaming narratives. For instance, reports might question the victim's behavior or attire, subtly suggesting that they contributed to the assault. Such portrayals not only harm victims by exacerbating their trauma but also influence public attitudes, reinforcing prejudiced beliefs about gender and sexual violence.

Conversely, media coverage has also played a crucial role in raising awareness about sexual violence and advocating for victims' rights. Investigative journalism and in-depth reporting have shed light on systemic issues within the criminal justice system and highlighted the need for legal and societal reforms. Campaigns and documentaries that focus on the experiences of survivors can foster empathy and understanding, challenging harmful stereotypes and promoting a more supportive environment for victims. The impact of media portrayal is thus double-edged, with the potential to either reinforce or challenge existing societal norms depending on the nature of the coverage (Bhalla, 2020)

Analysis of High Profile Cases

High-profile rape cases have had a profound impact on public discourse in India, often acting as catalysts for social and legal change. Cases such as the 2012 Delhi gang rape, known as the Nirbhaya case, brought the issue of sexual violence into the national spotlight and spurred widespread protests and advocacy. The brutal nature of the crime, combined with the media's extensive coverage, galvanized public outrage and led to significant legal reforms, including the introduction of stricter laws and faster trial procedures for rape cases.

Similarly, other high-profile cases, like the Kathua rape case and the Unnao rape case, have drawn national and international attention, further fueling public debate about the systemic issues surrounding sexual violence. These cases often expose flaws in the criminal justice system, such as delays in justice and corruption, prompting calls for reform and greater accountability. The intense media scrutiny and public reaction to these cases highlight the urgent need for comprehensive changes in both societal attitudes and institutional responses to sexual violence. Through these high-profile cases, the discourse around rape and sexual violence continues to evolve, reflecting a growing awareness and demand for justice and reform.

Psychological Impact on Victims

The psychological impact of rape on victims is profound and multifaceted, often leaving enduring scars that affect various aspects of their lives. Victims of sexual violence frequently experience a range of emotional and psychological responses, including post-traumatic stress disorder (PTSD), depression, anxiety, and feelings of shame and guilt. PTSD is particularly common, with survivors experiencing flashbacks, nightmares, and severe anxiety that can disrupt their daily functioning. The trauma of rape can lead to a deep sense of violation and loss of control, which may result in chronic emotional distress and difficulties in forming and maintaining relationships (Rimmer and Birch, 2019).

In addition to these immediate psychological effects, rape can have long-term consequences on a victim's mental health. Survivors often struggle with issues related to self-esteem and body image, as the assault can significantly impact their sense of self-worth and physical safety. Many victims also face difficulties in trusting others, which can lead to social withdrawal and isolation. The cumulative effect of these psychological challenges can impede a survivor's ability to lead a fulfilling life and achieve their personal and professional goals.

Societal Attitudes and Mental Health of Victims

Societal attitudes play a critical role in shaping the mental health outcomes for rape victims. In societies where victim-blaming and stigma are prevalent, survivors often experience additional layers of trauma. When victims are subjected to judgment and discrimination, it can exacerbate their feelings of shame and isolation. This societal stigma can discourage survivors from seeking help or disclosing their experiences, further intensifying their psychological distress.

The fear of not being believed or being subjected to invasive questioning and blame can prevent victims from coming forward, thereby hindering their access to support and justice. This lack of support can lead to increased feelings of helplessness and depression. On the other hand, supportive and empathetic societal responses can significantly aid in the recovery process. When communities offer compassion, understanding, and validation, it can help counteract the harmful effects of stigma and facilitate the victim's healing journey (Kazmi, Iftikhar & Fayyaz, 2023).

The availability and accessibility of mental health support and services are crucial factors in the recovery process for rape victims. In many regions, particularly rural areas, access to mental health services is limited, and there is often a lack of specialized support for survivors of sexual violence. Even in urban centers, while resources may be more available, they can still be insufficient to meet the demand and provide comprehensive care. Many victims struggle to access mental health services due to financial constraints, lack of awareness about available resources, or the stigma associated with seeking help. The shortage of trained professionals and the high cost of therapy can be significant barriers, preventing survivors from receiving the necessary care. Additionally, cultural and societal attitudes towards mental health can influence the willingness of individuals to seek help, with some communities viewing mental health issues as a personal weakness rather than a legitimate health concern.

Conclusion

Looking at the attitudes towards rape victims in India reveals a complex web of cultural, social, and psychological factors that deeply affect both individuals and society.

Historical norms, regional differences, and the impact of caste and religion all play significant roles in shaping how rape is perceived and addressed. A cross-cultural approach helps us understand the diverse experiences of survivors across various communities. It highlights the importance of tailoring support and interventions to fit different cultural contexts while still promoting gender equality and victim support.

Improving attitudes and support involves more than just changing laws—it requires a shift in societal attitudes. Raising awareness, combating stigma, and expanding access to mental health services are key steps. By creating a more empathetic and supportive environment, we can better uphold the dignity of victims and move towards a more just and inclusive society.

References

Beckmann, C. R., & Groetzinger, L. L. (1990). Treating sexual assault victims. A protocol for health professionals. Physician Assistant (American Academy of Physician Assistants), 14(2). https://pubmed.ncbi.nlm.nih.gov/10136535/

Bhalla, G. (2020). Why Lesser Rapes Are Happening In South As Compared To North India. IndiaTimes. https://www.indiatimes.com/news/india/why-lesser-rapes-are-happening-insouth-as-compared-to-north-india-524614.html

Evans, A. (2020). Why are North and South India so different on gender? The Great Gender Divergence. https://www.draliceevans.com/post/why-are-southern-north-eastern-indianstates-more-gender-equal

Hetu, V. (2020), "Public Attitude Towards Rape Crime and the Treatment of Its Victims in Delhi City", The Emerald Handbook of Feminism, Criminology and Social

Change (Emerald Studies in Criminology, Feminism and Social Change), Emerald Publishing Limited, Bingley, pp. 137-155. https://doi.org/10.1108/978-1-

Kazmi, S. M. A., Iftikhar, R., & Fayyaz, M. U. (2023). "It is all her fault": psychosocial correlates of the negative attitudes towards rape victims among the general population of Pakistan. Egyptian Journal of Forensic Sciences, 13(1). https://doi.org/10.1186/s41935-022-00320-3

Larsen, K. S., & Long, E. (1988). Attitudes toward Rape. The Journal of Sex Research, 24. https://www.jstor.org/stable/3812852

Olszewska, K., Piotrowski, P., & Wojciechowski, B. W. (2022). Attitudes Towards Rape and Their Determinants Among Men, Women and Non-Binary People in Poland. Sexuality & Culture. https://doi.org/10.1007/s12119-022-10042-2

Rimmer, B. and Birch, P. (2019), "Exploring factors affecting attitudes towards rape survivors: the role of sexuality and religiosity", The Journal of Forensic Practice, Vol. 21 No. 2, pp. 139-144. https://doi.org/10.1108/JFP-01-2019-0004

Singh, T. (2017). Young Adults' Attitudes towards Rape and Rape Victims: Effects of Gender and Social Category. Journal of Psychology & Clinical Psychiatry. https://doi.org/10.15406/jpcpy.2017.07.00447

Vohra, P. (2022). Attitude Towards Rape- A Comparative Study. International Journal of Indian Psychology, 10(2). https://doi.org/10.25215/1002.016

CHAPTER NINETEEN

Empowering Educators: Cultural Landscapes in the Classroom

- **Poorvi R**

Background

In this era of diversity in schools globally, teachers require cultural intelligence (CQ). The ability to adapt when faced with problems that result from interacting with community or objects from different cultures are known as Cultural Intelligence/quotient. The ability to operate effectively in international contexts represents a significant movement in study away from elucidating cultural differences and towards questioning how to bridge such disparities. Highly CQ teachers can understand and acknowledge people's cultural differences, communicate reasonably and develop curriculums that reflect the diversity of cultures. Also, they facilitate conflict resolution processes at the school level and enhance equity by ensuring equal opportunities for all learners. Traditionally, education systems were mono culturalist but globalization necessitated culturally responsive teaching. Teacher training programs as well as educational policies have changed over the past few decades since research indicated that those having higher levels of CQ are more effective.

As such, the relationship between cultural intelligence and teaching has shifted to putting more emphasis on student achievement, classroom environment and teacher-student relationships. Research shows that culturally intelligent teachers are better able to bond with their students leading to increased engagement and better classroom climates. Ongoing professional development in CQ is associated with enhanced instructional practices as well as adaptability. Consequently, they hardly find it difficult to create an inclusive learning environment where every child feels accepted and supported within a culturally diverse society.

This chapter emphasizes on cultural intelligence among the teaching groups of the society – among lecturers, professors and teachers and their ability to adapt and recognize diverse cultures. The Cultural Intelligence Scale was created to assess an individual's capacity for cultural adaptation. Regarding the CQS's dimensionality, construct validity, and uniqueness from other intelligences, studies on it have produced a mixed bag of findings. Based on the four-factor model urbanized, the conclusions of this study indicate (CQ) cultural intelligence among teachers.

Cultural Intelligence

Because of its current significance to globalization, organizational behaviour, and workforce diversity, Cultural Intelligence (CQ), or the capability to perform well in various cultural backgrounds and settings, has drawn more concentration from academics and professionals. Recent studies state that CQ accordingly predicts the various crucial outcomes and products of a global context, such as intercultural understanding, migrant performance, international standing, diplomacy, and multicultural group dynamics. A more complex kind of cultural sensitivity is called cultural cleverness (CQ), explained as "an outsider's capacity to understand someone's unfamiliar and confusing conduct in the same way that people from that society would". According to Livermore (2011), it is "the capacity to function successfully across a number of cultural contexts, such as ethnic, generational, and corporate cultures". The author of "The Cultural Intelligence Difference,"

Dr. David Livermore, emphasizes four practical components of CQ: namely – CQ Action, CQ Drive, CQ Knowledge and CQ strategy. CQ Action is the capacity to adapt your conduct to diverse cultures. It necessitates having a diversified and adaptable repertoire of reactions to fit various situations while keeping loyal to one. It is connected to the process of converting your goals and aspirations into actions in order to effectively communicate with people from various cultures. CQ Drive is the genuine interest and assurance in working well in culturally diverse environments. CQ Knowledge is the having an interest in discovering about various cultures and how they vary and on how they are identical. Acknowledging fundamental cultural differences and how they affect one and others. CQ Strategy is cultural diversity letting us pause and reflect on our own mental processes and judgements, as well as those of others.

Cultural intelligence incorporates four different basic factors, which include behavioral CQ, cognitive CQ, metacognitive CQ and motivational CQ. They are explained in the following ways: Metacognitive CQ is the capacity for mindful awareness of "planning, regulating, monitoring, and controlling" cognitive processes of thoughts and knowledge during intercultural conversations. Cognitive CQ includes "the knowledge, norms, practices, and conventions in different cultural settings". Motivational CQ is "the capability to direct attention and energy toward learning and functioning in intercultural settings" (Van Dyne et al., 2008), and behavioral CQ is "the capability to exhibit appropriate verbal and nonverbal actions when interacting with people from different cultural backgrounds"

In multi-cultural work environments, those who are able to make sense of intercultural experiences—for example, by passing judgement on their own and others' cognitive processes—make better decisions and perform better overall. The capacity to modify one's verbal and nonverbal conduct to meet certain cultural contexts allows for a flexible repertoire of behavioural responses that improves one's ability to execute a task in culturally varied environments. The performance increases when CQ-Strategy increases. Higher CQ-Behavior equals higher performance. Those who are curious about other cultures and comfortable interacting with individuals from other cultural backgrounds (CQ-Motivation) are better suited for environments where there is a wide range of cultural influences. Those who possess a wide range of verbal and nonverbal behavioural skills (CQ-Behavior) feel more at ease in circumstances that are characterized by cultural variety. The three different forms of adjustment all follow this pattern of relationships: General Modification, Interactional Modification and Work Modification

These four CQ elements, which have not before been applied to teachers, also seem to include the demands for cultural awareness and usefulness that are made of them in the writing. When used to describe educators working with children, we can claim that educators must have four different types of CQ: cognitive, metacognitive, motivational, and behavioural. Metacognitive CQ is the capability to assess those of one's pupil. It is also known as the consciousness of one's own misconceptions along with their assumptions. Cognitive CQ is knowledge of the norms, systems and values of one's students and their varied cultures. (Ang et al., 2007).

Review of Literature

Increasing awareness of cross-cultural interactions and illuminating individual disparities in performance in environments marked by cultural variety are the major aims of proponents of cultural intelligence. The theoretical underpinning for the inclusion of the cultural intelligence concept in professional discourse is the Sternberg concept of cognition, which places a focus on the multidimensional nature of intelligence and its functioning in real-life circumstances. The broadest definitions of cultural intelligence are the capability to successfully interact with people from different cultural backgrounds or the aptitude to adapt to new cultural conditions (Earley, 2002; Earley & Ang, 2003). According to Earley and Ang, cultural intelligence is a multidimensional concept that incorporates behavior, cognitive, metacognitive and motivational components (2003). The metacognitive aspect of cultural intelligence reflects the mental procedures people use to understand and learn about other cultures. Skills in planning, observing, and altering mental representations of cultural norms are essential. Those who are culturally savvy are cognizant of their personal cultural preferences, question cultural assumptions, and alter their thought processes both during and after interactions.

The cognitive component of cultural intelligence refers to understanding of cultural norms, customs, and behaviours gained via education and firsthand experience. Understanding the underlying foundations of cultural norms as well as the financial, judicial, and societal structures of many cultures is necessary for achieving this. High cognitive cultural intelligence people have an awareness of both differences and similarities in culture. The motivational aspect of cultural intelligence reflects the capacity to concentrate attention and effort on comprehending ethnic issues and navigating situations when they are prevalent. Due to their innate interest in and confidence in their capacity to perform in cross-cultural contexts, individuals who have a high degree of motivational cultural intelligence concentrate their attention and effort there. The behavioural aspect of cultural intelligence is the ability to interact with individuals from other cultures while using appropriate verbal as well as nonverbal clues. Based on their wide variety of spoken and nonverbal talents, communities with high levels of cultural intelligence in their behavior exhibit situational suitable behaviors, such as using facial expressions, gestures, tones and words that are acceptable for their culture.

The following results may emerge from effective intercultural contact: a) strong adaptation of a human being (manifestations in emotions of joy and welfare b) building along with sustaining positive relationships with people from various cultural ethnicities, and c) achievement in attaining the communication goals (Thomas, 2008). Moreover, he and colleagues stress that the core of cultural cleverness does not just lay in adaptability; as significant are a person's capacities to choose and/or modify their intellectual surroundings (Thomas, 2008). Experts who were looking for the most effective method of choosing people to employment overseas or in multinational organizations and even for a sound conceptualization of intercultural preparation, first became interested in the notion of cultural cleverness. Cultural intelligence has been studied and used most extensively in management and organizational psychology, but its potential applications are much broader and exist in all fields where it is necessary to comprehend the specifics of cross-cultural interactions and how they are regulated. Cultural intelligence has steadily gained importance in the educational setting as a result of the multicultural nature of modern classrooms.

In order for children to engage in this world which is more likely interconnected, it is now essential for academics and instructors to provide them the tools to communicate on a global scale (Friedman, 2005). Darling-Hammond (2010) asserts that while we deal with issues of justice, injustice and social fairness for children, this work begins in our classrooms. Children are more probable to start considering their selves as significant members of the community oh the whole when they discover the strength of their own voices and the relevance that one's own history and culture contributes to their classroom, town, and planet. As they continue to work with a student body that is becoming more and more culturally and linguistically diverse, teachers must address not just the educational and organizational demands of a task but also the intrapersonal and interpersonal demands of gathering the needs of learners on the whole. As a result, the roles of teachers are becoming more and more complex (CLD).

The rising body of educator-training resources for public school instructers that outline best practices for educating the CLD populations to get mainstreamed into their class environment also pushes for teachers to assume new roles as "cultural mediators" and "cultural brokers" and educators who "thoroughly comprehend dissimilar cultural systems" in addition to expecting them to comprehend the needs of their children linguistically. Similarly, instructors are expected to develop "sociocultural consciousness," that is often a responsiveness that aids in negotiating their contacts with their pupils while acknowledging that these communications are initiated by their sociocultural roots and grounds. They must understand that their experiences and origins have an impact on how they interpret the world (Banks et al., 2005). It is required of teachers to speak out for their children and eradicate learning inequities (Banks et al., 2005).

In her survey of CLD students working with their respective educators, Quintanar-Sarellana (1997) discovered that wilfully ignorant instructors are either aware of or not aware of the differences amongst their group of pupils and the cultural norms of the system of schools. They may also eliminate their children's culture subtly, but regrettably occasionally overtly. According to Alexander and Schofield (2006ab), instructors' implicit assumptions about their pupils frequently prevent them from receiving the academic support they require. The instructors who exhibit cultural awareness, on the other hand, are better able to comprehend their pupils and incorporate their cultures into the classroom. They are also more inclined to experiment with new teaching techniques and procedures. Also, they are more motivated to pursue personal and professional growth in order to interact with these students (Quintanar-Sarellana, 1997).

It was found that the use of cultural knowledge by educators to comprehend and approach their daily tasks with their students who were from various cultural roots was significantly more complicated and more complex than the idea of culture described in the four basic constructs of CQ used in this research, based on the examination of the teachers' perceptions of culture. Despite the fact that about nearly half of the educators that participated in this research expressed a certain level of resentment towards the ways in which additive culture was brought about and had been incorporated in the classrooms, they did notice the significance of the deeper levels of insofar that took place culturally as it gave a hand to their pupils in making associations to academics and facilitated authentic relationships with their students.

This research was significant because seven instructors described how they saw all of their pupils as culturally varied, with each one having their own culture that frequently included experiences from their past, family structures, and financial status.

Findings and Discussion

The main objective of this study was to examine the Cultural Intelligence (CQ) levels among educators in Karnataka, India. This was done by conducting a survey involving 79 participants aged between 21 and 60 years. Prior consent was taken from the participants. The respondents were made up of teachers from different institutions including lectures, school teachers, and professors who completed a demographic survey form on Google Forms consisting of 20-item four component Cultural Intelligence Scale (CQS). Respondents answered using the Likert scale which ranged from one to seven scales with high internal consistency (Cronbach's Alpha >

.70).

The findings of the study found out that teachers and educators have a moderate cultural intelligence and are discussed using descriptive statistics showing that male teachers had mean CQ scores of 107.32 (SD = 20.922), whereas female teachers reported mean scores of 100.44 (SD =18.930). It demonstrates that the gender difference in the departure from the mean for the samples is greater for females than for males. The t-value is -1.528 and has a significance level (.131) implying that there is no significant difference between males and females regarding their cultural intelligence scores as it appears in the table above suggests that gender does not seem to play an important role in determining cultural intelligence among educators in Karnataka based on this sample data set.

Limitations

This study has some limitations that include, the study's cross-cultural character prevents the establishment of a clear causation link between variables. Moreover, the research is cross-sectional while a long term one and test-retest approach would be more suitable. The sample for this study only responded to the questionnaire if they were in a teaching position at the moment. These findings may not be applicable to instructors who have retired. Acquiescence bias was inevitable in a self-report questionnaire. The question of whether these findings apply to certain groups but not all groups remain unanswered because researcher did not investigate various ethnic groupings within various geographical regions of India. Future research should take additional reports and objective facts into account.

Conclusion

Within the educational environment, teachers' presence of cultural intelligence or its lack can have a significant collision. The results of this study show that most instructors have a moderate degree of Cultural Intelligence (CQ). Given the instances that many instructors work in culturally diverse courses and are estimated to be able to fulfill all the requirements of their pupils from various cultural backgrounds and racial roots, which is a very encouraging finding. It also indicates that instructors who value cross-cultural interaction, see diversity in the classroom as a stimulant, and are receptive to cross-cultural learning score higher on the Cultural Intelligence Scale (CQS).

These research findings have much impacts on educator preparation. To boost future teachers' cultural quotient, the curricula for teacher training should include and encourage elements like intercultural receptivity, willingness to recognize and use cultural and multiculturalism variety as a learning supply (Petrovi, 2006), shared value, and mindfulness. Yet, the findings of this study suggest that exposure to individuals from various cultures and backgrounds is not a necessary prerequisite for fostering and growing of one's cultural intelligence. Participating in activities that involve close cross-cultural interaction is the greatest approach to build cultural intelligence. For instance, such actions ought to be made available through work and education in many cultures (Crowne, 2008), abroad trips for studies, national and international teacher substitute programmes (Petrovi & Zlatkovi, 2009), and other means.

References

Ang, S., & Van Dyne, L. (2015). Handbook of Cultural Intelligence: Theory, Measurement, and Applications. Routledge.

Ang, S., Van Dyne, L., Koh, C., Ng, K. Y., Templar, K. J., & Tay, C. (2007). Cultural Intelligence: Its Measurement and Effects on Cultural Judgment and Decision Making, Cultural Adaptation and Task Performance. Management and Organization Review, 3(03), 335–71.

Bücker, J., Furrer, O., & Weem, T. P. (2016, September 21). Robustness and cross-cultural equivalence of the Cultural Intelligence Scale (CQS). Journal of Global Mobility; Emerald Publishing Limited. https://doi.org/10.1108/jgm-05-2016-0022

Crowne, K. A. (2008). What leads to cultural intelligence? Business Horizons, 51 (5), 391-399.

Earley P. Christopher, Ang Soon. Cultural Intelligence: Individual Interactions across Cultures. Stanford University Press; Stanford: 2003.

Jameel, M. (2022, February 23). The 20-item, Four Factor Cultural Intelligence Scale (CQS). PSYCHOLOGICAL SCALES. https://scales.arabpsychology.com/s/the-20-item-four-factor-cultural-intelligence-scale-cqs/

Livermore, D. (2010). Leading with Cultural Intelligence: The New Secret to Success. New York: American Management Association.

MATSUMOTO, D. & HWANG, H.C. (2013). Assessing cross-cultural competence: A review of available tests. Journal of Cross-Cultural Psychology, 44 (6), 849-873. doi: 10.1177/0022022113492891.

MacNAB, B.P. & WORTHLEY, R. (2012). Individual characteristics as predictors of cultural intelligence development: The relevance of self-efficacy. International Journal of Intercultural Relations, 36 (1), 62-71. doi: 10.1016/j.ijintrel.2010.12.001.

N. G., K.Y., VAN DYNE, L. & ANG, S. (2012). Cultural Intelligence: A review, reflections, and recommendations for future research. In A.M. Ryan, F.T.L. Leong & F.L. Oswald (Eds.), Conducting multinational research: applying organizational psychology in the workplace (pp. 29-58). Washington, DC: American Psychological Association.

Petrovic, D. (2011, January 1). How do teachers perceive their cultural intelligence? Procedia - Social and Behavioral Sciences; Elsevier BV. https://doi.org/10.1016/j.sbspro.2011.01.076

REICHARD, R.J., DOLLWET, M. & LOUW-POTGIETER, J. (2014). Development of cross-cultural psychological capital and its relationship with cultural intelligence and ethnocentrism. Journal of Leadership and Organizational Studies, 21 (2), 150- 164. doi: 10.1177/1548051813515517.

STERNBERG, R.J. (1986). A framework for understanding conceptions of intelligence. In R.J. Sternberg & D.K. Detterman (Eds.), What is intelligence? Contemporary view points on its nature and definition (pp. 3-15). Norwood, NJ: Ablex.

Thomas, D. C., Elron, E., Stahl, G., Ekelund, B. Z., Ravlin, E. C., Cerdin, J., Poelmans, S., Brislin, R., Pekerti, A., Aycan, Z., Maznevski, M., Au, K. & Lazarova, M. B. (2008). Cultural Intelligence: Domain and Assessment. International Journal of Cross Cultural Management, 8(2), 123–143.

CHAPTER TWENTY

Cultural Currents: Awareness Among University Students

- **Sanjeev Prasad G**

Background

Cultural awareness is the foundation of effective communication and interaction in a diverse world. It involves recognizing and understanding the differences and similarities among cultures, encompassing values, beliefs, traditions, and customs. This awareness is essential in fostering mutual respect, inclusivity, and understanding in various social and professional contexts.

One of the primary components of cultural awareness is knowledge. This entails learning about different cultures, their histories, customs, and societal norms. By gaining knowledge, individuals can better understand the cultural contexts that shape people's behaviors and perspectives (Deardorff, 2006). This understanding helps in avoiding stereotypes and misconceptions that can lead to misunderstandings and conflicts. Second crucial component is attitude. Cultural awareness requires an open-minded and respectful attitude towards cultural differences. This includes being willing to question one's biases and assumptions, and being empathetic towards others. An open and respectful attitude fosters an environment where diverse perspectives are valued and included (Bennett, 2004).

Skills are also vital in cultural awareness. These include the ability to communicate effectively and appropriately across cultural boundaries. Skills such as active listening, empathy, and adaptability enable individuals to navigate intercultural interactions more successfully. Developing these skills involves practice and a commitment to continuous learning and improvement (Fantini, 2000). Self-awareness is the fourth component, involving an understanding of one's own cultural background and how it influences perceptions and interactions. By being aware of their cultural lenses, individuals can better manage their responses and engage more effectively with others (Byram, 1997). Cultural awareness is a multifaceted concept that involves knowledge, attitude, skills, and self-awareness. Together, these components equip individuals to engage respectfully and effectively in a diverse world, fostering positive relationships and reducing cultural misunderstandings.

In an increasingly globalized world, the concept of cultural awareness has gained prominence, especially among university students. Cultural awareness refers to the recognition and understanding of the differences and similarities between cultures, which includes values, beliefs, traditions, and customs. This awareness is crucial in fostering inclusivity, mutual respect, and effective communication within diverse environments (Deardorff, 2006). For university students, developing cultural awareness is essential as they prepare to enter a global workforce, navigate multicultural environments, and contribute positively to a diverse society.

Universities serve as microcosms of broader society, bringing together students from various cultural backgrounds. This diversity presents both opportunities and challenges. On one hand, it enriches the educational experience by exposing students to different viewpoints and cultural practices. On the other hand, it requires conscious efforts to promote cultural awareness and sensitivity to ensure a harmonious and inclusive environment. Institutions of higher education play a pivotal role in fostering cultural awareness. This can be achieved through curricular and extracurricular activities. For instance, incorporating intercultural communication courses into the curriculum can equip students with the skills needed to navigate cultural differences effectively (Fantini, 2000). Additionally, universities can organize cultural exchange programs, workshops, and seminars that promote intercultural dialogue and understanding.

Developing cultural awareness offers numerous benefits for university students. Firstly, it prepares them for the global workforce. In today's interconnected world, employers value employees who can work effectively in diverse teams and understand international markets. According to a study by Crossman and Clarke (2010), employers often seek graduates who possess cultural competence as it enhances their ability to work in multicultural environments and engage with clients and colleagues from different backgrounds. Secondly, cultural awareness enriches the educational experience. When students are exposed to different cultures, they gain a deeper understanding of global issues and perspectives.

This exposure broadens their worldview and fosters critical thinking. For example, courses that include global case studies and international examples help students understand the complexities of global interdependence and cultural dynamics (Leask, 2009).

Cultural awareness promotes social harmony and reduces prejudice. When students learn about and appreciate different cultures, they are less likely to hold stereotypes and prejudices. This understanding fosters a more inclusive campus environment where diversity is celebrated, and all students feel valued and respected (Gudykunst, 2003). While the benefits of cultural awareness are clear, promoting it among university students is not without challenges. One significant challenge is the existence of cultural biases and stereotypes. These biases can hinder open-mindedness and create barriers to effective intercultural communication. Educators and administrators must actively work to dismantle these biases through education and awareness campaigns. Another challenge is the potential for cultural misunderstanding and conflict. Even with the best intentions, cultural differences can sometimes lead to miscommunication and friction. It is essential for universities to provide support systems and mediation services to address and resolve such conflicts constructively.

Cultural Awareness

Cultural awareness is vital for university students for several reasons. Firstly, it enhances interpersonal relationships and communication within diverse environments (Deardorff, 2006). When students understand and appreciate cultural differences, they can interact more effectively and respectfully with peers from various backgrounds. Bennett (2004) emphasizes that cultural awareness not only involves recognizing differences but also valuing them, which leads to more meaningful and productive interactions. Moreover, cultural awareness prepares students for the global workforce. In today's interconnected world, employers seek individuals who can navigate multicultural environments and engage with diverse teams. Crossman and Clarke (2010) found that employers value graduates with cultural competence, as it enhances their ability to work in international settings and understand global markets. Therefore, cultural awareness is an essential skill for career success in a globalized economy.

Peer Interactions

Peer interactions also play a vital role in shaping cultural awareness. According to Astin (1993), the peer group is a powerful influence on students' attitudes and behaviors. Interacting with peers from diverse backgrounds exposes students to different perspectives and challenges their existing beliefs and assumptions. These interactions can lead to greater cultural awareness and sensitivity. Another critical factor is personal motivation. Students who are intrinsically motivated to learn about other cultures are more likely to develop high levels of cultural awareness. This motivation can stem from a genuine interest in other cultures, a desire to travel, or the recognition of the professional benefits of being culturally competent (Fantini, 2000). Therefore, fostering intrinsic motivation through encouraging curiosity and openness is essential for developing cultural awareness.

Interpersonal Skills

Developing cultural awareness has numerous positive outcomes for university students. One of the most significant outcomes is improved interpersonal skills. Students with high cultural awareness are better equipped to communicate effectively and build relationships with individuals from different cultural backgrounds (Gudykunst, 2003). This ability is crucial in both academic and professional settings, where collaboration and teamwork are essential. Cultural awareness also leads to personal growth and empathy. When students learn about different cultures, they gain new perspectives and develop a deeper understanding of the world. This process fosters empathy and compassion towards others, which are critical components of emotional intelligence (Goleman, 1995). Empathy enables students to relate to and support their peers, creating a more inclusive and supportive campus environment. Furthermore, cultural awareness enhances academic performance. Exposure to diverse perspectives can stimulate critical thinking and creativity, leading to better problem-solving skills and academic outcomes (Banks, 2008). For example, courses that include global case studies and international examples help students understand the complexities of global interdependence and cultural dynamics, which can enhance their analytical and critical thinking skills.

Despite its importance, promoting cultural awareness among university students is not without challenges. One significant challenge is the existence of cultural biases and stereotypes. These biases can hinder open-mindedness and create barriers to effective intercultural communication. Educators and administrators must actively work to dismantle these biases through education and awareness campaigns (Sue, 2010). Another challenge is the potential for cultural misunderstanding and conflict. Even with the best intentions, cultural differences can sometimes lead to miscommunication and friction. Universities need to provide support systems and mediation services to address and resolve such conflicts constructively (Ting-Toomey & Chung, 2012). Training students in conflict resolution and intercultural communication skills can also help mitigate these issues. Additionally, there is the challenge of ensuring inclusivity in cultural awareness programs. It is essential to recognize that cultural awareness is not just about understanding international cultures but also appreciating and valuing domestic diversity, including differences in race, ethnicity, gender, and socio-economic status (Gay, 2010). Universities must adopt a holistic approach to cultural awareness that encompasses all forms of diversity.

Student perspectives on cultural awareness are integral to understanding how effectively educational strategies promote intercultural competence. Numerous studies have explored how students perceive their own cultural awareness and its impact on their personal and academic lives. For example, Zhao, Kuh, and Carini (2005) found that students who engage in diverse interactions both in and out of the classroom report higher levels of personal development and satisfaction with their college experience. These interactions help students develop a more nuanced understanding of different cultures and improve their intercultural communication skills. Students also recognize the value of cultural awareness for their future careers. In a study by Salisbury, Umbach, Paulsen, and Pascarella (2009), students who participated in study abroad programs reported enhanced global awareness and a greater appreciation for cultural diversity, which they believed would be beneficial in their professional lives. These findings suggest that students are aware of the importance of cultural awareness and are motivated to seek opportunities that enhance their intercultural competence.

Several studies have examined the impact of specific cultural awareness programs on student outcomes. For instance, Engberg and Fox (2011) found that students who participated in diversity education programs reported significant gains in cultural awareness, empathy, and critical thinking skills. These programs often include components such as intercultural dialogue, reflective journaling, and community engagement, which provide students with opportunities to practice and develop their intercultural competence. Similarly, Jones and Abes (2013) found that living-learning communities focused on cultural diversity had a positive impact on students' cultural awareness and sense of belonging. These communities provide a supportive environment where students can engage with peers from different backgrounds and learn about diverse cultures through shared experiences and activities.

Implications

The main objective of this study was to examine the Cultural Awareness levels among University Students. This was done by conducting a survey involving 60 participants aged between 18 to 25 years old. Informed consent was taken from the participants. The respondents were undergraduate students of the University who completed the Cultural Diversity Awareness Questionnaire on Google forms with a Likert scale ranging from Never to Always (1 to 5). A higher score on the assessment indicates that you are acutely aware of prejudice and bias, and that you are very aware of the impact of your behaviour on others. Individuals who score high relate to others in ways that value diversity. A lower score on the assessment suggests that you are unaware of prejudice and bias, and that you are not fully aware of the impact of your biased behaviour on others. Individuals who score low communicate with others in ways that do not value diversity.

The t-test analysis conducted among 30 male and 30 female students at a University aimed to explore potential gender differences in cultural awareness. The descriptive statistics reveal that the mean cultural awareness score for males was 158.60 (SD = 60.193), while the mean score for females was slightly lower at 146.60 (SD = 55.339). The standard error of the mean for males and females was 10.990 and 10.104, respectively. To determine if the observed difference in mean scores between male and female students was statistically significant, an independent samples t-test was conducted. The Levene's Test for Equality of Variances indicated that the variances in cultural awareness scores between the two groups were not significantly different (F = 0.363, p = 0.549). Consequently, the assumption of equal variances was considered appropriate for the t-test analysis. The t-test results, assuming equal variances, yielded a t-value of 0.804 with 58 degrees of freedom. The corresponding p-value was greater than the conventional alpha level of 0.05, indicating that the difference in cultural awareness scores between male and female students was not statistically significant.

The statistical analysis suggests that there is no significant difference in cultural awareness between male and female students at the University. Despite the slightly higher mean score for males, the variation in scores within each gender group is substantial, and the overlap between the groups is considerable.

Limitations

The study's sample size was relatively small, with only 30 male and 30 female students. This limited sample may not adequately represent the broader student population at the University or other universities. Consequently, the findings might not be generalizable to all university students or to different cultural contexts. The study likely relied on self-reported measures of cultural awareness, which can be subject to various biases, including social desirability bias and recall bias. Students might have overestimated or underestimated their cultural awareness, which could affect the accuracy of the results.

The study employed a cross-sectional design, which captures data at a single point in time. This approach does not allow for the examination of changes in cultural awareness over time or the identification of causal relationships. Longitudinal studies would be needed to understand how cultural awareness evolves and what factors influence its development. The study was conducted at a single university, which may have a unique cultural environment that differs from other institutions. Factors such as the university's emphasis on diversity and inclusion, the cultural backgrounds of the student body, and specific campus initiatives could influence the levels of cultural awareness. Therefore, the results may not be applicable to institutions with different cultural contexts. The study did not account for potential confounding variables that could affect cultural awareness, such as prior intercultural experiences, participation in cultural exchange programs, or specific courses on cultural competence. These factors might have influenced the results and should be considered in future research.

Conclusion

This study aimed to investigate gender differences in cultural awareness among university students in a University. Analysing the cultural awareness scores of 30 male and 30 female students, the findings revealed no statistically significant difference between the two groups. While male students had a slightly higher mean score (158.60) compared to female students (146.60), the t-test results indicated that this difference was not significant, suggesting that gender does not substantially influence cultural awareness levels among the students sampled.

The absence of significant gender differences in cultural awareness has important implications for educational strategies and initiatives aimed at fostering intercultural competence. Since both male and female students exhibited similar levels of cultural awareness, universities can design and implement programs to enhance cultural competence uniformly across the student body. This approach ensures that all students, irrespective of gender, are provided with equal opportunities to develop the essential skills needed to navigate and succeed in an increasingly globalized world.

While this study offers initial insights into gender differences in cultural awareness among university students, the limitations highlight the need for further research. Future studies should aim to include larger and more diverse samples, employ longitudinal designs, use validated measures of cultural awareness, and consider a broader range of demographic and contextual factors to provide a more comprehensive understanding of this important issue. By addressing these limitations and expanding the scope of future studies, educators and policymakers can develop more effective strategies to promote cultural awareness and intercultural competence in higher education.

References

Astin, A. W. (1993). *What matters in college? Four critical years revisited.* Jossey-Bass.

Banks, J. A. (2008). *An introduction to multicultural education* (4th ed.). Pearson.

Bennett, M. J. (2004). Becoming interculturally competent. In J. Wurzel (Ed.), *Toward multiculturalism: A reader in multicultural education* (pp. 62-77). Intercultural Resource Corporation.

Byram, M. (1997). *Teaching and assessing intercultural communicative competence.* Multilingual Matters.

Crossman, J. E., & Clarke, M. (2010). International experience and graduate employability: Stakeholder perceptions on the connection. *Higher Education,* 59(5), 599-613.

Deardorff, D. K. (2006). Identification and assessment of intercultural competence as a student outcome of internationalization. *Journal of Studies in International Education,* 10(3), 241-266.

Engberg, M. E., & Fox, K. (2011). Exploring the relationship between undergraduate service-learning experiences and global perspective-taking. Journal of Student Affairs Research and Practice, 48(1), 85-105.

Fantini, A. E. (2000). A central concern: Developing intercultural competence. *SIT Occasional Papers Series,* 1-32.

Gay, G. (2010). *Culturally responsive teaching: Theory, research, and practice* (2nd ed.). Teachers College Press.

Goleman, D. (1995). *Emotional intelligence: Why it can matter more than IQ.* Bantam Books.

Gudykunst, W. B. (2003). *Bridging differences: Effective intergroup communication* (4th ed.). Sage Publications.

Jones, S. R., & Abes, E. S. (2013). *Identity development of college students: Advancing frameworks for multiple dimensions of identity.* Jossey-Bass.

Leask, B. (2009). Using formal and informal curricula to improve interactions between home and international students. *Journal of Studies in International Education,* 13(2), 205-221.

Salisbury, M. H., Umbach, P. D., Paulsen, M. B., & Pascarella, E. T. (2009). Going global: Understanding the choice process of the intent to study abroad. Research in Higher Education, 50(2), 119-143.

Sue, D. W. (2010). *Microaggressions in everyday life: Race, gender, and sexual orientation.* Wiley.

Ting-Toomey, S., & Chung, L. C. (2012). *Understanding intercultural communication* (2nd ed.). Oxford University Press.

Zhao, C. M., Kuh, G. D., & Carini, R. M. (2005). A comparison of international student and American student engagement in effective educational practices. The Journal of Higher Education, 76(2), 209-231.

CHAPTER TWENTY-ONE

Unifying Cultures: Insights and Reflections

- Likitha S

How cultures reflect and outline an individual's psychological process is a fascinating aspect. Culture is the most visible aspect such as dress, wealth, religion, emotions, perceptions, marriage, music, communication, understanding the concept of self, etc. Knowing how culture influences people in different aspects of life is a quintessential phenomenon that provides insight into understanding people's perceptions. Cross-cultural psychology analyses these behaviours across various cultures and perceptions globally. For instance, one study suggested a strong relationship between gender and individualism-collectivism in self-concepts especially regarding family values and social relationships which was observed in collectivist cultures (Watkins Adebowale Akande et al, 1998).

Studies by Kitayama, S., & Markus, H. R. (1994) examine how culture plays a vital role in one's emotions and extensive studies have been conducted to explore and understand how culture impacts the development and shapes one's personality as well as emotions. It was stated that beliefs and values shape an individual's conscious experience. It was also said that biological contribution is much greater and plays an essential role in understanding the aspect of culture and emotion. It is so fascinating to discover that emotions can be perceived and interpreted so differently across various cultures. This could be understood through various aspects, marriage rituals across South Asians are very different yet one common aspect which can be observed is the approval from their families which is not seen in Western cultures. Intercultural and interracial marriages are on the rise globally and it is substantiated in chapter three. Intercultural marriages require getting accustomed to that culture which can be challenging. It may need patience and effective communication for marriage to work. Coming from two different cultures, partners will have differences in interpreting the same situation from various perspectives which could create conflicts. Overcoming these requires acceptance of each other's cultures and respecting them. Falicov, C. J. (1995) in his Clinical Handbook of Couple Therapy, elaborately explains different cases of interracial marriages and the challenges faced by them. One case highlighted the cultural differences in a married couple and how stereotypes impacted their marriage. Expression of emotions plays a vital role and the variations are seen in different cultures across the world.

Media is playing a pivotal role in highlighting these pop cultures, and their norms. The K-pop genre has taken over the world recently and has been trending ever since. Not just K-pop but K-drama, clothing style and cuisine too.

Many adolescents have been trying to keep up with the Korean culture and their mannerisms. When compared, there is a vast difference between South Korean and Western cultures. Chapter one explores the relationship between media and how significantly it is shaping different cultures like fashion, skincare, music, TV programmes etc and has changed the perceptions of the public. From influencers to celebrities, each and everyone is aware of the trending things across the world. These intercultural things could be seen in other trends too. Apart from pop culture, media exposes the stereotypical aspects and how people perceive mental health in several cultures. It is a known fact that a lot of stigma surrounds mental health, especially seeking help or being open about one's issues which leads to shaming. Again, when compared between Asian and Western cultures, some individuals prefer traditional healing over other ways which has been rightly pointed out in chapter four. For instance, in India seeking treatment for a mental disorder is considered taboo and is surrounded by stereotypes. Not just in healing but manifestation of disorders is influenced across different ethnic groups. There have been studies that state that different patterns are seen across the lifespan in various nations in many age groups (Schönfeld, P., Brailovskaia, J., & Margraf, J. (2017).

The impact of culture is vast across the world with thousands of aspects. When discussing menstruation or sex openly in a public gathering, one is criticized as it is still considered taboo and is shunned. India is a country with 1.45 billion population and a vast culture (The Hindu, 2024). There are various religious practices across India when it just comes to menstrual practices which have their taboos and perspectives as stated in chapter fifteen. Despite its shortcomings, the media is debunking the myths that surround menstruation in India as it has been shrouded, which led to misinformation and stigmas. It has been breaking taboos and creating awareness about menstrual hygiene.

Interpretations about mythology state numerous definitions and theories that explain the cross-cultural aspect of things and human behaviour which shape their beliefs and values that have evolved over centuries. Theories and interpretations have been drawn from mythologies, like Ramayana for example. Ramayana highlights the good- Rama and Sita, the bad-Ravana and Kaikeyi, loyalty- Hanuman and Lakshman and the intricacies in interpersonal relationships. The relationship between Rama and Sita is the central theme which explains the exile, abduction and societal expectations. These relationships enlighten the human nature and its ethics. The characters and their interactions serve as examples of life teachings and complexities of human nature. Different cultures have unique norms, practices be it marriage ceremonies or death rituals. Variations have been observed across the globe when it comes to mourning and honouring the dead.

Understanding different cultural practices concerning everything and anything can help society function in a better way. It can help professionals comprehend numerous concepts related to culture, and bring in new perspectives and interpretations. Collectively examining the mythological aspects of Ramayana, myths that revolve around the perception of rape and menstruation, deliver insights into enduring the identities and complexities of human behaviour which can help in building an equitable society. It can help in forming new norms and interventions for the betterment of the world. Creating awareness about countless cultures and their norms also provides insights into how one can communicate with them which in turn aids in maintaining society's well-being.

References

Falicov, C. J. (1995). Cross-cultural marriages. Clinical handbook of couple therapy, 231246.

India's population to peak in early 2060s to 1.7 billion before declining: United Nations July 2024 retrieved from India's population to peak in early 2060s to 1.7 billion before declining: United Nations - The Hindu

Kitayama, S., & Markus, H. R. (1994). Introduction to cultural psychology and emotion research. In S. Kitayama & H. R. Markus (Eds.), Emotion and culture: Empirical studies of mutual influence (pp. 1–19). American Psychological Association. https://doi.org/10.1037/10152-010

Schönfeld, P., Brailovskaia, J., & Margraf, J. (2017). Positive and negative mental health across the lifespan: A cross-cultural comparison. International Journal of Clinical and Health Psychology, 17(3), 197-206. https://doi.org/10.1016/j.ijchp.2017.06.003

Watkins Adebowale Akande James Fleming Maznah Ismail Kent Lefner Murari Regmi Sue Watson Jiayuan Yu John Adair Christopher Cheng Andres Gerong Dennis McInerney Elias Mpofu Sunita Singh-Sengupta Habtamu Wondimu, D. (1998). Cultural Dimensions, Gender, and the Nature of Self-concept: A Fourteen-country Study. International Journal of Psychology, 33(1), 17–31. https://doi.org/10.1080/002075998400583